Craft Business Basics

How to Start and Operate

A Successful Home-Based

Craft Business

Craft Business Basics

How to Start and Operate

A Successful Home-Based

Craft Business

Terri Anderson

Contents

CHAPTER 6

CHAPTER 7

CHAPTER 10

OTHER WAYS TO PROFIT FROM YOUR DESIGNS.................. 128

RESOURCES.. 139

PREFACE

I began crafting at age five, as soon as I could manage a pair of knitting needles! A well-meaning aunt introduced me to the art of knitted potholders, and thus began a love of crafts that continues to this day.

As I grew up and grew older, I continued to craft and never met a craft I didn't like. I tried everything that appeared in each month's craft magazines that arrived in my mailbox and often found myself modifying the original design, or redesigning the piece to suit my own taste.

After learning and experimenting with the many fiber arts including needlepoint, cross stitching, and crochet, along with learning many other crafts throughout the years, I kept coming back to the idea that it would be great to somehow make money from my efforts. What could I make and sell that would pay me back for my time and efforts? Would it be possible to actually make a profit from designing and selling my crafts?

I finally found the answer at a bead show where the multitude of dazzling beads and pearls were too enticing to pass up. I purchased some of the beads and supplies, along with a book about how to make jewelry, went home and went to work. Within a weekend I had created a few pieces that I took to work on Monday. One of my coworkers admired my work and told me about an upcoming craft show that I should apply to. As they say, the rest is history. My business, Heavenly Designs, was born and continues to grow each year as I continue to design and sell my work.

Many have asked what it takes to start up in the craft design business, and I hope this handbook will share some information that I've learned along the way that will make your journey a little easier and enjoyable. Good luck and happy crafting.

INTRODUCTION

The craft industry is booming with sales of craft products exceeding video rentals. The Hobby Industry Association (HIA) annual survey states that sales in the U.S. craft industry rose to over $10 billion dollars in the late 1990's! Attend any well-known craft show on a Saturday morning and you will see first hand how popular this industry has become.

Do you dream of awakening each day and bouncing out of bed, excited about what the day may hold for you? Do you envision only having to go as far as the other end of the house or yard as your commute to work? Do you want to use your time each day as you choose, and not because it is mandated by a boss? Are you creative and always thinking of another way to make something look better? If you answered yes to these questions, then owning and operating your own craft business may be just what you're looking for!

But before quitting your day job, let's look at some of the behind the scenes views of the life of a crafter and designer. Crafting can be a way of utilizing your inner resources, expanding your creativity and serving as a release from the pressures of daily life. But you must recognize the difference between crafting for love and crafting for money before making the decision.

CRAFT BUSINESS BASICS

Starting your own business includes opportunities as well as risks. The benefits include generating personal wealth from your efforts, as well as the sense of freedom from being your own boss and making your own decisions. But you will also be losing the security of a regular paycheck, a predictable work schedule, fringe benefits, paid vacations and a retirement plan. Also, having your own business involves risking your property, your health and even your pride. You must take all of this into consideration before making the jump.

CHAPTER 1

WORKING AT HOME

Do You Have What It Takes?

Do you have what it takes to start and manage a new business? Although optimism and enthusiasm go a long way, it is a fact that more than half of all businesses that are started each year end up failing within the first three years of their existence. Most of these business owners felt their failure was due to the economy, too much competition, government regulations and other factors. But a study by Dun and Bradstreet found that most small business failures occurred because the business did not offer exactly what the customer wanted, failed to make changes in their business to meet a changing marketplace, or lacked knowledge about how to operate the business from a standpoint of legal, financial, purchasing, accounting or marketing matters.

You can beat the odds. Successful business owners tend to have qualities that make them stand out from the crowd:

➢ They are opportunity seekers. They are always looking for new and different ways to meet the needs of their customers.

➢ They look to the future. They envision three to five years ahead and prepare to capitalize on any opportunities that may become apparent.

➢ They commit to be the best. Customer satisfaction is the most important element to their business.

➢ They are realistic. They know there is no such thing as a free lunch, and don't try to take shortcuts to make a fast buck.

➢ They are tolerant of doing the small details as well as the big sales. They know the business requires the mundane in order to survive and thrive.

➢ They are able to bounce back. They know that a setback isn't the end, but a learning experience.

How do you rate yourself with the above elements? Starting a small business is not a casual undertaking, but if you want to take the challenge, you must do whatever you can to improve your chances for success.

Honestly answer the following questions to see what your strengths and weaknesses are before you decide whether or not to start a home-based craft business:

❑ I can make decisions, even if they're the wrong ones.

- ❑ I can handle rejection and criticism without giving up.

- ❑ I am organized and enjoy being on top of things.

- ❑ I like to take charge and see things through to completion.

- ❑ I like people and tend to get along well with most.

- ❑ I will work hard for something I want and believe in.

- ❑ I have "stick to it ness" and will continue with something no matter what.

How many of the above can you honestly answer "yes" to? Just because you may have a negative answer to one of the above questions doesn't mean you won't succeed in your own small business. But it does give you something to consider and otherwise plan for. If you begin by knowing your weaknesses, and can adjust accordingly, your chances for survival are much greater.

Many small businesses fail within the first five years of their existence. These failures occur for any number of reasons, both business and management related to personal reasons. But whatever the reason, the statistics don't give much hope to small business owners. It is therefore, your responsibility to be sure you don't enter into that category of statistics.

Information and resources exist today like never before. There are more ways to find answers to your questions than you can even begin to imagine. Books and magazines, organizations, newsletters, and Internet technology can pretty much get you whatever you need. Don't wait to try to figure a problem out on your own. Seek help as soon as you know you have a problem and move forward toward success.

Pros and Cons

One of the biggest advantages of having a home-based business is that you are able to work at home. And one of the biggest disadvantages of having a home-based business is that you are working at home!

Let me explain. First of all, being able to work at home saves money. Commuting expenses, meals, clothing, and childcare are cost savings when you work at home. Working at home allows you to toss in a load of laundry, run the dishwasher or start cooking dinner whenever you want. But these benefits can easily become disadvantages as they distract you from doing what you need to do to be successful in your business. Professional tasks must be separated from personal tasks when you work at home. Everything that needs to be done can be done with proper planning and organization, and we'll discuss how to do this later on.

Most who choose to work from home do so because they want to be home with their children. How wonderful to not have to worry about day care and sickness each day. But being home with your children all day can often become so much of a distraction that no work can be done at all.

If you don't learn to manage, control and organize interruptions and distractions, you can end up becoming a full-fledged procrastinator, always saying you can't get anything done. If you can't get your work done, you can't be successful in your own business, so you must learn to modify your lifestyle and priorities up front.

Take a hard look at yourself as you read through the following sections and see how your personality type will function and react as a business owner and wearer of many hats.

Business or Hobby

The first thing you must decide is if you want to own a business or have a hobby. A business requires work, whether you're in the mood, sick, tired or any other excuse. A hobby is something you look forward to doing for relaxation. You can pick and choose when you want to do it. Businesses can be rewarding, but not all aspects of it are fun. Businesses provide income and have some advantageous tax benefits that we'll discuss later on.

The IRS also has some ideas about the difference between a hobby and business, and it's very important to determine which you are very early in your career. The IRS requires proof that the goal of your business is to make money. Their guidelines state that you must show a profit at least three out of five years.

You are defined as being self-employed when you net more than $400 per year, which requires you to file a Schedule C, declaring your self-employed income when you file your federal income tax return whether you own a business or have a hobby. So if you intend to have a business you must diligently work to prove it, because if the IRS doesn't agree, it can disallow otherwise legitimate business deductions.

Ask yourself the following questions to determine if you are a hobbyist or a business professional:

- ❑ Do your business documents including business cards, letterhead, and brochures have a professional appearance?

- ☑ Do you maintain a business checking account and credit card?

- ☑ Do you make a profit with business earnings?

- ☑ Do you maintain a bookkeeping system and ledger for all income and expenses?

☑ Do you have all the necessary permits and licenses to operate a home-based business?

☑ How much time do you devote to your business?

☑ Do you file a Schedule C for business expenses and deductions?

☑ Does your office or studio space reflect a place of business?

Unless you can answer "yes" to the above questions, you may not be viewed as a legitimate business.   Be sure, as you read through this handbook, to do what is necessary to establish yourself as a true business professional.

Working Alone

The one question everyone starting a home business should ask is whether they can handle the solitude. Although being able to work at home with the job you love may seem like the American dream, the reality may end up being entirely different. No matter how glamorous it sounds, working at home every day all alone or only with small children or the dog to talk to can be boring. It is often hard to maintain motivation and enthusiasm for your work when the afternoon soap operas are beckoning.

Many find out quickly that they miss daily contact and interaction with others. Some have become depressed and unable to work at all, and have chosen to return to traditional employment.

One of the best ways to combat loneliness is to remind yourself that you're alone because you chose to be. You're alone because your work allows you to be independent, and to pursue your passion for what you do for a living. If you can find fulfillment in your aloneness, you will be able to overcome the loneliness.

Some of the best ways to be alone, but not be lonely are to:

➤ Stay connected. Meet other crafters for lunch. Join a home-business owners group or craft association and attend their meetings. Do occasional or scheduled volunteer work. Make a deliberate effort to be with others on a regular basis.

➤ E-Chat. Join in scheduled chats on the Internet on business issues or topics you are interested in.

➤ Get out of the house. Go to the library every Tuesday and Thursday afternoon. Join a health club or go for a walk. Visit a bookstore. Make getting out of the house a part of your daily routine.

➤ Find a hangout. A coffee shop or ice cream parlor, or luncheonette, or any place where you can become a "regular".

➤ Get a pet. Having another living, breathing creature around can be comforting. A dog will listen to you tirelessly, and will never contradict a word you say. They will give you an excuse for a break, and will be only too happy to be your best friend when you need one.

➤ Have an enjoyable office. You will be spending a lot of time there, so be sure you enjoy being there. Make your office attractive and comfortable so you'll look forward to spending time in it. Add background noise. Play soft music or talk-radio. Often just having voices in the house can be enough to ward off emptiness.

I must admit to having had an adjustment period when I first began working at home. But I quickly modified my schedule to allow some social interactions each day, which was all it took. I try to spend an hour each afternoon, during my down time, to read craft materials, journals, articles or any other materials that I come across. This gives me enough of a motivational boost to want to keep doing what I'm doing. Additionally, I have a friend who is also a jeweler and we have a monthly lunch date to discuss shows, designs, ideas, and anything else.

One of the main advantages of having a home-based craft business is the many hats we must wear. The variety of tasks that need to be done by a business owner helps to prevent boredom. Between designing, manufacturing, marketing, ordering materials and supplies, selling, bookkeeping, and all the other business tasks needed for a successful business, there is rarely time to become bored. Even when all alone.

Maintaining Motivation

Working alone at home can create a lack of motivation. Constant creation and production, along with all the other business tasks that are required, can become tedious. To succeed, think of ways to make your work fun. You need to be happy while at work to want to stay with it.

Many at home business owners and crafters discover a device that keeps them motivated. Some play music, while others promise themselves a reward for completing a certain number of tasks. I know one crafter who's husband thought she was crazy for wasting her time with this "little business". Her motivation was to prove him wrong. The last I spoke with her, she had made a net profit of over $35,000 for her previous years sales. Not bad!

My motivation is similar and very simple. Money motivates me to do whatever is necessary to keep my business moving forward. As I complete my work, especially if I've finished several designs and have added them to my inventory, I can mentally calculate my profit. This is enough to inspire me to do more, and I usually do.

Find whatever it takes to motivate you. Work hard to stay motivated and keep producing products while maintaining business details. When you begin selling your finished work, you will be glad you did.

Balancing Business and Personal Life

If you have a family, a home-based business is going to somehow affect it. Additionally, your family will also affect your business. How you deal with these two interplaying forces will tell how successful you will be in balancing business and personal life.

In the beginning, be sure to include family members in the details of the business. Involve them in discussions and try to value their input. Of course, small children will not have the same ideas of what the business will or should be like as older children and spouses or significant others. But you should still try to get them onboard at the onset, so they will feel their cooperation is important to your success.

It will be important for you to let family, friends, neighbors and everyone else know that you are serious about this business. Even though you are at home, you will still be working, and unavailable for anything not related to the business. Often people think because you work from home you are free to do anything you choose, from picking up packages to shuttle service. Until you lay the foundation that you are at work and cannot be interrupted, your life will be out of balance.

Another factor is to keep both home and business completely separate from one another. When you are "home" and not working, be sure you are truly paying attention to your family, just as you pay complete attention to business when you are working. If you can clearly show friends and family the distinction between your working life and your personal life, you will have a much better chance of success.

Work hard to establish a business routine and stick to it. When others know your schedule, they will be less inclined to disturb you at other times.

What's Holding You Back

Many potential craft business owners are full of reasons why they cannot succeed. I will often see a beautiful handcrafted item and ask the person where they got it. When they respond that they made it themselves, I want to know if they're in business. If they aren't, I try to encourage them to start. But the reasons are endless.

Do you use any of the following excuses?

❑ I work full time and don't have any time for a home-based business. This is an oldie but goodie. We all have the same amount of time each day, and must choose how to use it. We'll talk more about time management and priorities later, but for now it's enough to know that if you want to start a home-based business you have the choice of working on your business or watching TV. You can decide what's most important.

❑ I don't have the start-up money. It really doesn't take much to start a small business. Most crafters are already producing products anyway, and just haven't taken the leap to selling them as a business. But if you need money, there are creative ways to get what you need if you're willing to look.

❑ I don't have any extra room to use as an office / studio. I often tell my children, where there's a will there's a way. I know crafters who operate from an RV, and you can't get much smaller than that.

❑ I'm too old, too young, handicapped, have children, undereducated...(you get the idea). Regardless of what you perceive your handicap to be, you still have the potential to do whatever you choose to do. You may have to work a bit harder, but if you are serious and willing to devote yourself, you can succeed.

❑ I'm afraid I won't succeed. Fear of failure is probably the number one reason people won't try something. Fear and worry are enough to stop most in their tracks. But you'll never know how successful you can be unless you try.

You only have one shot at this game called life. Take a chance on yourself and see how far you can go. Maybe you will have to make adjustments and changes to reach success, or maybe it will find you without your even trying. But whatever happens, at least you're in the game!

CHECKLIST - Working at Home

- ❑ Have you decided to operate as a small business and not a hobby?

- ❑ Are you willing to do whatever it takes to make your business successful?

- ❑ Are you comfortable working alone?

- ❑ Are you self-motivated?

- ❑ Is your family supportive?

- ❑ Can you overcome any fears or objectives and get started today?

CHAPTER 2

MAKE IT LEGAL

Choose A Name

If you are sure you want to have a business, there are several decisions that must be made before you hang out your shingle. First you must create a business identity, which includes a name and a legal status.

In choosing a business name you should consider the following five points:

1. The name should be meaningful. It should tell customers something about you. Your business name is a marketing tool that can become a powerful form of identity and recognition. Many craft designers use their own names as their business name. This can be useful in personalizing your product or business, especially if your name is unique or unusual.

2. Be sure the name you choose is easy to understand and pronounce. A short, memorable name is better than a long, difficult to remember name.

3. Be sure to choose a name that can grow with you and your business identity. My friend, Linda Glass, was designing stained glass and using the business name Linda's Glass. This worked well for her until she became interested in designing needlepoint.

4. As we'll discuss later, your business name, unless it exactly reflects your own legal name, will have to be registered. As no two businesses in the same geographic area can legally operate with the same name, you should come up with several choices. The more unique, the better your chances of getting the name you want most.

5. Don't rush. Try out your new name before registering for business licenses and ordering business cards. Ask other's opinions and take their collective advice.

Remember that deciding on a business name should be fun. You will be spending a lot of time with this name, so take your time and choose wisely.

Type of Ownership

After deciding on a name it will be time to make your business legal. Most businesses operate in one of three legal forms of organization. You must decide whether you will operate as a sole-proprietor, a partnership, or whether to form a simple corporation. Each business owner needs to understand the characteristics associated with each type of ownership so you can select the most appropriate one for your individual business. Let's look at some of the benefits and disadvantages of each.

Sole Proprietor

A sole proprietor owns the entire business and is totally responsible for the success or failure of the business. The legal implication is that since the owner has sole control over the business, the owner also has sole responsibility including legal and financial liability. This means that any liability that results from operation of the business extends directly to the owner and is not limited to the business. This is the major disadvantage or risk of this type of ownership.

In a sole proprietorship, all business income is taxed as personal income. When your federal income taxes are prepared, all that is required is a Schedule C showing profit and loss from the business. The net income or loss is added or subtracted to any other income that is reported on the tax return. Since this is the easiest form of business ownership to form and operate explains why nearly 75 percent of all businesses in the U.S. are sole proprietorships.

Carefully weigh what your liabilities are with regard to your craft. Can the liability be covered by insurance? Speak to your attorney before committing.

Partnership

A partnership is a form of business having two or more owners. They exist when at least two people combine their ideas, talents and capital for business purposes in a legally binding manner. A partnership is similar to a sole proprietorship in that legal and financial liabilities are extended to all partners. Should the business default, the lender can look to the partners to satisfy any outstanding bills. For tax purposes, partners are taxed on their share of the business profit or loss at their individual rate as personal income.

As the success rate of partnerships is very low, it is wise to consult with an attorney to iron out the legal details at the onset. The partnership agreement should include how profits and liabilities will be divided, each partner's rights and duties, and what will happen to the business in the event of withdrawal, termination, or death of a partner.

Partnerships must be registered in the county where the business will be located. Check with your local government offices to see what other requirements may be needed.

Corporation

A corporation is very different from the above types of legal entities in that the corporation is treated separately from its owners. This means that the liabilities of the corporation may not be passed on to the owners, but are limited to the amount that is invested in the corporation. Unless you are required by a bank or other lender to personally cosign for the corporation, your liability is limited to whatever you have invested into the corporation.

Although incorporating seems appealing because of the legal and financial liability, they do have some disadvantages. It costs more to form a corporation, and corporations take more time and paperwork to create and maintain. Taxes are also more complicated and costly when filing as a corporation.

There is a special type of corporation that may appeal to small business owners called the "Subchapter S." This is a relatively easy corporation to form and one of the major advantages of this type of corporation is that it is taxed like a proprietorship instead of a corporation. The corporation doesn't pay federal corporate income tax, but the stockholders report their share of the corporate profits on their tax return.

There are many things to consider when choosing the legal status for your business. When starting Heavenly Designs, I considered all the above information and decided to have a sole proprietorship. Jewelry doesn't have a very large liability, and the liability I may encounter at craft shows can be covered by insurance. I'd rather pay insurance than have the hassles of a corporation. But every business is unique and different and you should contact your attorney and C.P.A. to get assistance in setting up your business so it will best benefit your individual needs.

Fictitious Name

Unless the name of your business is your full legal name, first and last, you will need to file a fictitious name form. If you don't file for a fictitious name you can be Jane Brown's Portraits, but you cannot be Jane's Portraits or Portraits by Jane.

Contact the Secretary of State's office for an application. When you submit the application and filing fee, they will conduct a search to see if any other business with the same name exists in the same county. If so, you will have to go back to the drawing board to choose another name. If the business name is not currently in use, it becomes yours and can be renewed every five years.

After filing you must publish the name and information about your business in several consecutive issues of a local countywide newspaper. This "Affidavit of Publication" lets the public know who you are and what you're doing as a new business.

Business Licenses

Another important legality is to determine whether you will need a city or county business-operating license in order to conduct business from your home. Many local governments generate tax revenues from businesses, even those that are home-based. Because I live within the city limits, I needed both a city permit as well as a county license. So be sure to check at your local City Hall to obtain any permits or licenses.

Insurance and Banking

Be sure to check with your insurance agent to see if your homeowner's or renter's policies will cover your business equipment and supplies, as well as finished products. A portion of your tools may be covered, but only up to a certain amount. If your equipment is costly, you may need to get a rider to provide added coverage. Also check to see about your liability coverage. If customers will visit your home, be sure you have adequate coverage should someone trip and fall.

Check on your vehicle insurance, especially if you plan on using your vehicle for business purposes. If you have thousands of dollars of inventory you are transporting to a show, will it be covered if you should be in a bad accident and it is destroyed.

Other insurance you may want to consider would provide coverage for your goods at craft shows as well as liability should your canopy blow down and cause damage or injury.

Other insurances you need to consider as a home-based business owner includes health and disability insurance. How will you pay your bills if you become too ill to work or disabled? And don't forget life insurance if you are responsible to anyone else for financial support.

Check to see if an umbrella policy would take care of all your needs. In today's litigious society, you must be prepared for every possibility.

As for banking, once you have filed for a fictitious name or business license you can open a business bank account. Take documentation with you to verify your business is legitimate.

A separate business bank account is not an option. The IRS will not accept a business operating from a personal checking account. First of all, a real business has its own bank account. A hobby can exist with a personal bank account. This is one of the best, and easiest ways to prove your business is truly a business and not a hobby. Secondly, the IRS frowns on "commingling of funds." If audited, they may disallow legitimate deductions if paid from a personal checking account.

Department of Revenue

The Department of Revenue is responsible for collection of sales tax. As a business owner you are not required to pay sales tax on any materials that you will resell. You will be required to pay sales tax on what items you sell. Registration is painless and inexpensive (in Florida). For only $5.00 I was legally able to begin charging sales tax on my merchandise as well as not having to pay sales tax on supplies I purchased that would be resold. Visit your local office to register and get complete details and information.

Home Occupation Use

Don't be surprised when you apply for your business license to be handed an application for a Home Occupation Use Permit. This permit, costing anywhere from $25 to $200, outlines most of the same conditions covered by a business license. Each city establishes the number and conditions of this arbitrary fee.

Many think this added tax is a disincentive to the very people who help decrease congested roadways and increase the tax base of their cities by working at home. Many call it double taxation.

Zoning Variances

Most housing developments are zoned for residential use, and businesses are zoned for commercial use. If you want to use your home for business purposes, you may have to apply for a zoning variance. You can contact your city planning commission to find out the zoning status of your home and what it will cost to obtain a variance.

Finally, be sure to check with your homeowners association about any covenants and restrictions regarding home businesses. Many times, if there are restrictions, you can explain that your business will not have any impact on the neighborhood and gain permission from the board.

I began Heavenly Designs as a sole-proprietor. My business plan included designing jewelry for sale as well as selling my designs. In setting up the business, my first stop was to the Secretary of State's office to file for a Fictitious Name. After a quick search and paying the fee, my business name was registered for the next five years. My next stop was to the Department of Revenue to establish an account to pay sales tax. Within a couple of hours, including travel time, I was officially a business.

CHECKLIST - Making It Legal

- ❑ What will the legal status of your business be? Sole Proprietor, Partnership, or Corporation?

- ❑ Have you filed for a Fictitious Name? A Business License?

- ❑ Have you opened a business checking account?

- ❑ Have you filed with the Department of Revenue to collect sales tax?

- ❑ Have you checked on zoning requirements for a home-based business?

CHAPTER 3

TAXING CONSIDERATIONS

All About Taxes

There are several kinds of taxes that you will have to become informed about as a small business owner. Tax laws are very complicated and tend to change often, so it's advisable to have a knowledgeable specialist such as an accountant or CPA help you get started.

First, check to see what local taxes you may be responsible for, if any. Some states and local governments may impose an inventory tax on business equipment and product inventory. This could include items you have ready for sale but are not yet marketing.

State and Sales Taxes include Income Tax, Sales Tax, and if you have any employees, Unemployment Tax. Most states have an income tax, which is calculated on your net profits. It is usually due when you file your Federal Income Taxes on April 15 or sooner. I live in Florida, which is one of the few states that don't have an income tax. Local sales taxes may also be required, so be sure to do your homework to be sure you pay everyone you are required to pay.

Another requirement is a Resale Tax Number. Anyone selling products in a state that collects sales tax will need to get a tax number from the State Department of Revenue. We'll discuss this in more detail later, but for now it's important to know that you will need to register and collect sales tax on any finished products you sell to customers. You will have to submit this tax to the state on a regular basis – usually quarterly.

Federal Taxes are probably the most involved taxes you will have to do, and expert guidance will save you headaches as well as money. An accountant will be able to tell you whether you need to file and pay Estimated Tax Payments that are required for self-employed individuals. These are taxes that are paid quarterly, based on estimated earnings. There are penalties for not paying these when due, and for underestimating them. So get an accountant to help you figure out what needs to be paid.

At the beginning of this book we looked at whether you were conducting a business or pursuing a hobby. This becomes very important at tax time.

The IRS says you are a business if you:

☑ are sincerely trying to make a profit,

☑ are making regular business transactions, and

☑ have made a profit at least 3 years out of 5.

Other factors include how much time you devote to your business, the way you keep your business records, and the way you present yourself to the public. If the IRS feels you don't meet their criteria, your "business" will be ruled a "hobby" and any losses deducted on your taxes will be disallowed. Hobby income is still required to be reported, but expenses can only be deducted up to the amount of income, and any losses can't be claimed.

Finally, you will have to pay Social Security Taxes when your profit reaches a certain level. You will then have to file a Self-Employment Form along with your income tax, and pay into your own personal social security account. The wage base and rate are continually being recalculated and increased, so check with your accountant or the IRS to learn the current rate. You should also request a statement of earnings each year to be certain your deposits were posted to your account. Contact the Social Security Administration to request a Summary Statement of Earnings and send it off to get proper verification of your earnings and deposits. I keep the verification from year to year in case there is ever a discrepancy.

Bookkeeping 101

Begin your business and make your tax preparation easier by setting up a good bookkeeping system. Although it's ok to be creative when designing and crafting, the same doesn't hold true for business practices. You may choose to keep your records in simple ledger notebooks or on a computer. How you keep your records is not as important as the fact that records are being kept.

Receipts and invoices must be kept to confirm expenses and income. Cancelled checks do not satisfy IRS requirements. An accountant will help you set up your bookkeeping system on a columnar pad. These come in many sizes and with varying numbers of columns. The simpler the better, whenever possible.

I use a very simple method to keep track of my expenses. I keep a double-entry notebook on my desk with an envelope labeled "receipts" tucked in it. Each time I make a purchase I record the purchase in the notebook and put the receipt in the envelope. When a page of entries is complete I put a corresponding number on the top of the page and the same number on the envelope. I then start a new envelope for the next page. So at the end of the year I may have pages numbered 1 through 5, and envelopes numbered 1 through 5 containing the receipts for each page. Should I ever encounter an IRS audit, I will have all of my receipts to substantiate each claimed expense.

Another tool you will need for tax planning as well as for knowing how you are doing financially is a profit-and-loss statement. This accounting document will measure and predict your business operation by looking at the net sales you make minus expenses. This will give you an accurate view of where you stand in financial terms. Because this form becomes more valuable as the business grows and ages, it is important to be as accurate as possible when entering profit and expenses.

A balance sheet is another important document that you will need to become familiar with. This form will give you a picture of your business assets and liabilities. As a new business this form may not provide much help, but as the business grows it will be useful to look back and see how you've progressed.

The final and most important financial item you need to understand is cash flow. Cash flow is more than just your net profit. It essentially shows how money moves in and out of your business. It shows all the income received and expenses paid, and the timing of each. If you want your business to succeed you will have to be able to have a steady flow of income into the business to pay expenses and to provide an income.

Cash flow documents are similar to profit-and-loss statements with the exception of the cash flow report showing after-tax profits.

It is important as a small business owner to become accustomed to using proper business forms and terms, and learning what is necessary to complete them accurately. If you understand where you are, financially, you will have a better idea of where you want to go.

What Is Deductible?

All business expenses are deductible. This means that whatever money you spend on supplies, materials, resources, or anything pertaining to your business can be deducted against your earnings when you file your federal income taxes.

As you begin to make purchases, look at the following list to be sure you don't overlook a deduction that you are entitled to.

- ☑ Office equipment and supplies

- ☑ Craft supplies

- ☑ Marketing and advertising

- ☑ Permits and licenses

- ☑ Insurance

- ☑ Taxes

- ☑ Postage

- ☑ Improvements to home-office

- ☑ Studio improvements

- ☑ Costs related to photography

- ☑ Wages you pay for help

- ☑ Fees you pay for accounting, legal, taxes, consultants, etc.

- ☑ Dues to belong to professional groups

- ☑ Subscriptions for magazines and journals

- ☑ Educational classes and materials, including travel expense

- ☑ Phone (including cell phone) and fax lines for business purposes only

- ☑ Mileage (keep a notebook in your car and document ALL business related travel)

- ☑ Home-office use

Home office use is one deduction that seems to make many small business owners cringe. The home-office deduction seems to raise more concern that any other.

Basically, the IRS allows home-based businesses to deduct a percentage of their mortgage or rent payment, real estate taxes and utilities on the percentage of space they use exclusively for business purposes.

In order to claim this deduction you must use the room fully and completely for business. It cannot serve as a spare guest room or for family storage. You can't clear off the dining room table and claim the deduction for that space. All non-business furniture and personal possessions must be removed.

If you do use a portion of your home exclusively for business, you can determine what percentage of the total square footage is for business use and calculate a deduction of that percentage for all home-related expenses. Get IRS Form 587 (Business Use of Your Home) for more information.

This isn't a deduction to be afraid to take as long as you are legitimately using the space for business purposes. You should not have any problems if your home is the primary location of your business, you spend most of your working hours there, and you use the space exclusively for business.

I converted an unused living room into an office / studio. This space is 22 percent of the total square footage of my house. You will see a desk, work table, computer, printer, fax and copy machine, bookcases, chairs and filing cabinet in this room with no other personal furnishings. I use the room exclusively for designing and manufacturing, writing, and meeting with customers. I claim deductions of 22 percent of my mortgage and utilities for my home office / studio.

As you can see, there are many tax advantages to having a business instead of a hobby. But the key is to be aware of what you are legally entitled to claim, to remember to claim everything, and document with receipts. If you maintain a simple bookkeeping system you will not only know exactly how your business stands financially, but will also be prepared for end of the year tax preparation. Take time at the startup of your business to set up your tax structure and bookkeeping system. Get the advice of a CPA. It will be money well spent down the road. And when tax time comes, and it will, you will be prepared.

CHECKLIST - Taxing Considerations

Business Bookkeeping

➢ Have you set up your accounting and bookkeeping system?

➢ Do you understand what you will need to do and what to keep to satisfy the IRS?

➢ Have you researched what other taxes may be required?

Selecting an Accountant

➢ Ask if they deal with small businesses

➢ Get referrals from existing clients, and check them

➢ Know exactly who you will be dealing with

➢ Find out up front how much you will be charged for services

CHAPTER 4

DEVELOPING YOUR

BUSINESS PLAN

Where Do You Want Your Business To Go?

The difference between a dream and a goal is a plan. Even though you may not think a business plan is necessary, doing one will help you to focus on precisely what you want to do and what you expect from your business. By organizing your business on paper, you can begin to conceptualize your business in a real way.

There are several good reasons for taking the time to do a business plan. By researching and writing your goals down on paper, you will have a clear picture and direction for your business. This will make future decision making much easier as the business evolves and progresses. Should you need a loan for start up costs, a business plan is required. Banks like a clearly organized document, not a vague estimate or thoughts. And those who wish to hire you for your design expertise or products may also want to see your business plan to assess if your business is legitimate.

A good Business Plan will state goals and objectives. It will help you develop your marketplace niche and help you reach your goals in a logical sequence.

The reasons for writing a business plan are somewhat different for the home-based crafts business than for many other start-up businesses.

Often, your reason for developing a business plan will be more fundamental and will help you to consider the following:

➢ Is the venture you are considering a feasible one? Can you convince both yourself and others that what you want to do can be successful?

➢ What are your strengths and weaknesses? Will they allow you to accomplish what you want to?

➢ What about your financial resources? Where will you get the funding you will need to get started and keep going?

➢ Who are your future customers? Mom is nice, but you will need others to succeed.

➢ What is your timetable for starting and operating your business? Is it feasible?

➢ How will you know what to set your prices at? Will customers pay what you're asking?

➢ Will you have the time management ability to complete the work necessary? Do you know your short and long-term goals?

➢ Can you identify business trends that could affect your business?

➢ If needed, can you get financing from a financial institution?

You need to consider these items at the start, before ever putting pencil to paper. After having a general idea of how you could respond to the above, then you can begin the planning process.

What Should Your Plan Look Like

There are many books available on creating and developing a business plan and I would recommend you get one or two from the local library or bookstore and go through them. But there are a few basic elements that should be included in every plan.

➢ Product Development – what do you make to meet your customers' needs and desires?

➢ Marketing – how will you let customers know what you have?

➢ Sales – how will you persuade customers to buy from you?

> ➤ Operations – what are the day-to-day activities of your business?

> ➤ Personnel – will you hire others and how will you manage?

> ➤ Finance – how will you project and measure your profit and loss to see how you're doing?

> ➤ Management – how will you get all of the above done in a way to accomplish your goals?

Other things that must be considered in your plan include what you will need to get started. What resources and materials will be required at the business onset? Think about what you will need to do, step-by-step, to make your business become a reality. And finally, how will you know if you are making progress?

The first page of your business plan should be the **Title Page**. It should provide the name of your business and the date.

The **Executive Summary** should follow, which will give a brief overview of your entire plan in one or two pages. It should include what you want to do, a statement of your purpose and mission, your goals and how you plan on reaching them.

Next will come the **Table of Contents**, which will be done after your complete document is completed with page numbers.

Chapter 1. The Business, will begin the main body of your plan. This is where you'll explain if the business is a new start-up or an existing enterprise, and about the products you will sell. Additionally, you will need to tell why your products are better than the competitions, and explain your goals for the business. The following should also be included in this chapter:

a. Legal Structure

State whether your business will be run as a sole proprietorship, a partnership, or a corporation.

b. Owner Information

State your full legal name, address and phone number as the owner of the business.

c. Personal History

State your qualifications and experience and include a copy of your resume.

d. Type of Business

State the exact nature of your business. "Crafts" is too broad a term. Explain whether you design, manufacture, exhibit or write about crafts.

    e.   Business Objective

        Clearly state the purpose of your business other than to make money.

Chapter 2. Product Description / Products Offered will come next. Here you will describe your work in detail, starting with specific products you will sell, and then including added value. If you want to exclusively design crafts, then include photos and copies of your designs. You can include photos of your products. Added value is what makes your products special to the customers such as cultural or religious influences.

Chapter 3. Market Description / Industry Data is where research enters the picture. The more you know about the industry you are entering, the better your chances of success. This is where the demand for your products will be analyzed. Start by looking at any trends concerning your medium in the craft industry, and how they may affect your business. Then define your target audience by telling about your customers...where they live and work, how they will use your products, their buying habits, and all other information you have gathered. Tell the size of your market and its expected growth. Finally, discuss your location and how your product fits with where you plan to sell them.

Consider the following:

a. Product Benefit
Begin by answering the question, "Why would someone buy my product or service?" People buy things for benefits. What will be the benefit to someone by purchasing your product?

b. Statistics
This is essentially part B of your research. Study how big the industry is that you want to enter. Look at trade journals and gather facts and figures to support your findings.

c. Other Supporting Data and Attachments
Because others are doing the same thing you want to do, you will be able to build credibility on your idea. This is a good thing. If others are successful, you have a good chance of following in their footsteps. So clip articles from trade and consumer publications relating to your industry and insert them here.

Chapter 4. Marketing Plan / Approach to Selling. Here you can explain your method for sales. Be as specific as possible in detailing the selling side of your business. There are four primary sections included in your marketing plan. As this is the heart of your business, be sure to spend some time researching and completing this section.

a.   Who are your customers? Learn all you can about them.
     Find out their income levels, their social and educational
     levels, and their occupations. Determine how they will
     learn about your product or service, and why they should
     buy it. How will you know they want or need your product
     or service? Decide whether they will pay your price.

b.   What are your marketing strategies? How does your
     product fit into the existing market? How did you arrive at
     your price? What is the risk in trying your product? Will it
     require any training and are their any government
     regulations with regard to its use? What customer service
     strategy will you use as a follow-up? What will be your
     sales strategy to reach your target market and how will you
     get your product to the customers?

c.   What marketing research techniques will you use? Will you
     interview your customers or survey them about your
     product? Will you talk to other business owners with
     similar interests? What makes your product different /
     similar to those already being marketed? What can you
     offer that is not already being done?

d. What about your competition? Who are they and where are they located? What are their strengths and weaknesses? What are yours? What can you learn from them?

Chapter 5. Production Process is where you will describe how you make your products. It should tell what your raw materials are and the equipment needed, along with the methods and time involved for completion. The operations section will explain quality control, inventory management and how you will deal with vendors.

Chapter 6. Management and Personnel is where to explain who else will be involved in your business and what role they will have. Will you have any employees or partners? How will others affect the daily operations of the business?

Chapter 7. Financial Data / Budget Proposal should start with the financial proposal. This chapter will be vital if you plan on borrowing any money, so be sure to include sufficient detail. You should explain what you want to do with your start-up money and provide a balance sheet outlining planned overhead and income. You should include a copy of your past 3 years tax returns if requesting funding. List everything you need to purchase and the estimated cost for each item. Estimate what your monthly operating expenses will be and propose what your cash flow statement will look like.

Your **Summary** should summarize the preceding chapters. It should restate your business objectives and explain what you hope to accomplish within your business. You may also want to include documentation about the following:

a. Proprietary Rights

   Copies of any copyright forms, trademarks, logos or patents would go in this section.

b. Outside Contracts

   If you have a licensing agreement with another company, a rental contract or lease agreement, or any other legally binding document, list it in this section.

c. Future Growth

   State any plans you may have for future expansion of your business products or services. State what you hope your business will look like in the future.

Attachments and Appendices is the final section of your plan. Here you should list and number all documents you are including in you business plan such as any photocopies, articles, resumes, references, endorsements, photos, market studies, etc.

Although preparing a business plan is a lot of work and may seem overwhelming, it will be time well spent. Don't omit this phase in establishing your business as it will provide a foundation for what you want to accomplish.

CHAPTER 5

DEVELOPING YOUR MARKETING STRATEGY

Market Research

Market research is used to identify and describe the current and future market for a particular product. It looks not only at the product, but also at the customer, the competition, and any outside forces like the economy, to see what the effects on a business may be.

Many times, crafters make products to please themselves rather than offering something to please the customers. It is much easier to fill an existing need than to create a new market, and you should always be considering this when deciding what to produce.

There are some questions you should ask to help define the market for your products:

- In 50 words or less, what am I trying to sell?

- Why do I think my product will sell?

- Is it something customer's need, or something they want?

- Why might they buy it if they don't need it?

- What is the profile of my customer? (Male or female? Young or old? Professional? Etc.)

- Where are my customers located and how can I get to them?

- Is my product already being produced or mass-produced?

- Is there a demand for my product?

- Will the market for my product expand? If so, how soon?

- What will my competition be like?

- Is my product better than the competition? Why?

- Is my product different from the competition? Why?

- How does my competition sell, advertise, publicize?

- If there isn't any competition, why?

After considering all of the above you will be able to best position your business so customers will perceive you in a certain way. You will have thought about what business you're in and what your strengths and weaknesses are compared to the competition, and you will be able to state why your product has value and why it should be purchased. By properly positioning, or repositioning your business you build an image in the minds of the customer that inspires them to do business with you. You give an implied promise of a benefit, and become known by that promise or benefit.

Pricing Strategy

Novice business owners, through ignorance, fear or lack of confidence, often price their products much less than the market price. This hasty decision, made because of lack of research and information, often ends up being an expensive mistake resulting in failure.

Many beginning crafters feel they must have rock bottom prices and undercut their competition in order to succeed. But they don't realize they are only hurting their chances of success, not helping them. If you set your prices lower than the competition, buyers may think your products aren't as good and won't want to purchase the "cheaper" item. You are the new kid on the block, whereas the other crafters have established a reputation and a following of satisfied customers. But having low prices means you have to produce more product just to keep even with the others, so you'll be working twice as hard and having to sell twice as much. Only you can answer if it's worth it or not.

The opposite may occur and you may want or need to charge more for your products. Perhaps you use better quality materials or your assembly is better. If this is the case, be sure you tell it. Don't let customers wonder why you have higher prices than the guy three booths down. Tell them why.

One of the best decisions you can make is to work with your competition instead of fighting them. Crafters within a given community can be a tight knit group, often knowing and working with each other for years. You are the newcomer to this group.

Your competition can be your best friend or your greatest enemy and the choice is yours. I have always kept the Golden Rule as a guiding principle for my personal and business lives, and always looked to my competition as a friend and source of help and guidance. I have never been disappointed. In turn, I try to help as many new crafters as possible, and have been rewarded in unimaginable ways.

Whatever you decide, be sure your prices are set based on a firm market analysis and not on a hasty decision. We'll discuss pricing some more in Chapter 6. Making a Profit.

Niche Marketing

A niche is a small corner that you comfortably fit into that is easily overlooked by others. If you can find a niche for your crafts business, your chances of success increase. So what can you do to stand out from the rest? Is there something you do or can offer that will make you special? Do you have an expertise in a particular area that others are lacking?

Begin by looking at what you offer to see if it can somehow be modified to benefit a different market segment. When I first began my jewelry business I made angel pins. Well, pretty soon everyone and their mother began making angel pins. So I began adding small charms to my pins, like golf clubs for the golf enthusiast and seashells for the beachcomber. Before I knew it, I had created a small niche market selling "charm angels". Although I now have progressed to designer jewelry, people still look for, and I still make, charm angels.

Your Marketing Plan

The marketing plan you develop now will help guide your business in the future. You thought about it when preparing your business plan, and gathered some information, and the marketing plan you do now will further enhance your business plan.

The following questions can be used as an outline for your marketing plan. Answer each question in as much detail as possible, and when you are finished you will have a complete, detailed analysis of the best way to proceed with your business.

1. What do I do?
    Describe your business in 25 words or less.

2. How does my product benefit buyers?

   Customers buy benefits, not products. What does yours offer?

3. How do I want customers to perceive my business?

   How do you want to be recognized and known?

4. What does my target customer look like?

   What is their age, income, location, lifestyle, etc.?

5. Who is my competition?

   Describe your competitors. How much of the market do they have? What are their strengths and weaknesses? How would they get your business?

6. How will I sell my products?

   Will you sell retail or wholesale? Will you sell directly to customers at craft shows or otherwise, or will you sell through stores and consignment? Will you sell mail order, on the Internet, or at trade shows?

7. How will I promote and advertise my products?

   Will you put ads in craft magazines or other publications? What other ways can you promote yourself and your products?

8. What are my selling policies?

   Will you offer a guarantee or other customer satisfaction terms? Will you offer discounts at any time? What is your shipping and delivery policy?

9. Is my pricing within a reasonable range?

   How do your prices compare with the competition? Can you make a reasonable profit based on your current prices? Can you justify higher or lower prices than the competition? Does the current economy support your prices?

By now you should get the idea. Having a good marketing plan is like looking into the future success of your business. You will have a detailed roadmap of where you want to go, along with all the directions to help get you there.

Like a business plan, your marketing plan will change and evolve over time. You can't just do it once and expect that it is now finished forever. Consider both your business plan and marketing plan a work in progress. As your product line changes and your customer base changes, and as you grow and develop as a crafter, you will need to revise and update your plans.

Marketing is something you will have to do throughout the life of your business. You can't stay ahead of the competition unless you are constantly trying new ways to market and developing new ideas for promotion and advertising. This is an ongoing challenge.

So go in with an open mind, realizing that things will change, but change is a good thing. As long as you know and expect to continually be modifying what you do, you will remain a step ahead.

CHECKLIST

Marketing Strategy

- Have you conducted sufficient market research?

- Is there a niche market you can fit into?

Marketing Needs

- What will you need to get started?

❑ Artist Bio	❑ Logo
❑ Brochures	❑ Photos of Products
❑ Business Cards	❑ Portfolio
❑ Catalog	❑ Promotional Postcards
❑ Envelopes	❑ Resume
❑ Fliers	❑ Slides / Transparencies
❑ Letterhead	

CHAPTER 6

MAKING A PROFIT

Three Elements in Profit

Now that you've set up your business and organized your office, you're ready to begin making and selling your products. If you're like most small business owners, your primary motivation in operating a business is to make money. The bottom line is what you hope will be an amount that fairly compensates you for your time and effort, after you've covered the costs of raw materials. You can make the most if you pay attention to the three basic elements in profit:

1. Purchase

2. Production

3. Price

First of all, you will gain the most profit if you can purchase your supplies and materials at a discount. Secondly, you must work efficiently and consider time into your production costs. And finally, you must price your products effectively so they will sell. Let's look at each of these elements in more detail.

Purchase

There will be a big difference in the amount of profit you can realize depending on where you purchase your supplies and materials. You may, at first, purchase supplies from local stores at retail prices. If you do this, at least be sure to provide the store with a copy of your sales tax certificate so you won't have to pay sales tax on your raw materials.

Retail purchases are fine if you are looking for a special item and only need a very small quantity. But remember that when you purchase retail, the store is also making a profit, and so must charge you more, which decreases your profit when you sell your product.

What you will want and need to do as soon as possible is to begin making wholesale purchases. There are many companies that will sell raw materials at wholesale prices without having to order hundreds of dollars worth, and your challenge is to find these suppliers.

Begin by asking other crafters in your medium where they purchase their raw materials. I've found that crafters in general are very helpful to each other, especially if they know you're just starting out. I have found out about many supply sources as well as local bead shows from fellow crafters, and have been able to purchase my materials at much reduced prices.

The Internet is a wonderful resource for finding what you need. Do a search of your raw material and see all that comes up. But be careful and be sure you are dealing with a reputable company. Request a catalog and begin by making your first order small enough to meet their minimum. Then you can judge timeliness and product quality before making a large investment.

Wholesalers usually require some proof that you are a business. Normally, your tax certificate for resale will suffice.

Production

How your product is produced can have an impact on your profits. Often, making only one item at a time is not cost-effective. If you make many of the same item, you need to learn to make them in batches. Figure out what steps in the production process can be done at the same time, and do a batch at a time.

For example, one of my designs is for angel pins. Each head, wing, halo and face must be glued on individually, and the glue left to dry for several hours before gluing on another part. I begin by laying out my designs, as I may use different pieces for wings, bodies, etc. After I have designed about a dozen angels, I begin by gluing all the wings to the bodies. When they are dry, I glue the faces on and again leave them to dry. I repeat the process until everything is glued, and I then have a dozen individual angel pins that were all completed at the same time.

This method doesn't always work so easily, but there are still ways to increase and improve on production. I also design beaded jewelry, each a one-of-a-kind design. I used to design, string, price, label, and finish each piece from beginning to end. But I discovered my mind comes up with other designs as I'm working on an existing project. So instead of ignoring my inspiration and perhaps loosing the idea, I now keep several designs in progress at the same time. I will even stop in mid-design to begin another project if I get a good idea. Then after I have several pieces on beading boards, I string each of them at the same sitting. I then proceed to price, label, and enter each into my inventory. This, for me, is much more efficient and productive, and I end up with four or five finished items instead of one.

Do you use one color of paint for one process and another color for the next? Don't spend time changing paint after each piece. Instead, do what needs to be done with the same color on several pieces at the same time and then change colors.

Planning is the key to successful and profitable production. Planning will help you make the most of your time and efforts, and will give you the best profit margin for your business.

Learning to be efficient is an ongoing process, but one that will pay off in time-savings and ultimately profit if you commit to looking for ways to do things more effectively.

Price

Before you can set a price on a product, you must consider the costs of your raw materials, your labor, and any overhead or selling costs. Just as retail stores add overhead store costs into their retail prices, you should think about what expenses you have that will have an impact on your profit.

Some expenses to consider include long distance phone charges, magazines, books, subscriptions, craft show fees, memberships, office supplies, postage, utilities, car use, insurance, licenses, equipment, bank fees, and any other items. Even though these things are tax deductions, they still impact your bottom line.

Although there are many formulas for calculating how to price an item, you are the only one who knows how much the raw materials cost, how much time it took you to design and create the piece, and how much of your expenses include overhead. So only you can set a selling price that will let you recoup your expenses and make a profit.

Many new crafters start out by pricing their merchandise too low. They are so happy that someone likes their product enough to buy it that they don't pay attention to the fact that they're losing money until it's too late. They usually end up working like crazy to make more and more products, spending more and more money, and then wonder why if they are selling so well they don't seem to have any money! Discouraged, these crafters soon give up, not always realizing what went wrong.

So let's look at a few "rules of thumb" to get started pricing your work. Wholesale pricing is when you sell your product to someone who will resell it at retail. If you sell to any shops or stores, they will want to pay wholesale.

A simple rule for calculating a product's wholesale price is to double the cost of the retail price. This is a very oversimplified formula that assumes your overhead can be covered in doubling your costs for raw materials.

When looking at setting prices, you can see why it's so important to keep your production costs down. You may decide you can't afford to sell a product wholesale, because it will not sell at a high enough price to give you what you need.

I discovered early on that I could not sell my angel pins wholesale. The pins cost an average of $5 to make, and I could make a dozen in a day, but angel pins only sell for $8 to $10 retail at craft shows, so stores can't mark them up and sell them for $16 to $20 when I'm selling them for less in the same general location.

Think creatively of different ways to increase profit.   Is there any way to package your product into sets of merchandise?   I often sell sets of jewelry items to include a necklace, bracelet and earrings.   I slightly reduce the price of a combination of pieces, but increase my overall profit.   It's always good to be able to offer a matching item and a discount if they purchase both pieces.   My discount is around ten percent on the price of the second piece, which is rounded to the nearest dollar. It ends up being a nice discount for the customer while increasing the size of my sale.

There are many ways to increase your sales and profits and you will discover even more ways to save money and reduce costs as you become more experienced.   But the important thing to remember is to keep your bottom line in sight.   If you're in this for the money, be sure you don't lose your focus along the way.

Pricing For Profit

There are several additional factors that you must consider when deciding what to charge for your products.   We've briefly discussed pricing for the wholesale marketplace, but must also consider retail pricing in the equation.   There are certain costs that must be figured in to the cost of your product in order to get a clear idea of your exact profit.

Direct costs must be taken into account when you produce any craft. The money spent on materials, supplies and other products to make the product must be calculated.

Overhead costs must also be figured in. These include all the other things that you may not realize, but are expenses that must be paid for somehow. Utilities, mortgage or rent, office supplies, equipment and depreciation are all things that cost you money, and unless they are added in to the price of the product, you are not earning what you think you are. Anything that is not a direct expense for materials or labor would be figured in here. A rule of thumb is to calculate overhead as 33.3% of the direct costs. So if my direct costs are $5.00, my overhead would be $1.66.

Labor is the final factor that must be considered. Your time has value, and it is a cost of the manufacture of the finished product.

A simple equation for determining price is the following:

Materials + Overhead + Labor + Profit = Price

So based on this formula, if I spend $5 for materials, and figure overhead at $1.66, and labor at $10 per hour for 2 hours would equal $20, and my profit would be two times the above total or $26.66, I should price my item at $53.32.

At this time I have to ask myself if my product would sell at this price in the marketplace I am in. If so, no problem. But if not, I need to carefully consider what my approach will be. Can I reduce costs to lower the price? Is my pricing unrealistic? What do my competitors do and how much do they charge?

Experience is the best way to come up with solid selling prices. Look at what others are selling similar products for, and decide if yours are better, more intricate, use better quality materials, and have more detailed designs. If so, charge a bit more. And if yours are more simple that the competition, charge a bit less. But stay aware of the competition as well as what your costs are in relation to what your prices are.

CHECKLIST - Making a Profit

Pricing Costs to Consider

- ☑ Materials and Labor

- ☑ Overhead

- ☑ Profit

Rules of Thumb

- ➢ Labor and materials shouldn't exceed 1/6 of the Retail Price or 1/3 of the Wholesale Price

- ➢ Wholesale is 3x the materials and labor

- ➢ 1/3 of Wholesale is Profit

- ➢ 1/3 of Wholesale is Overhead and Marketing

Overhead Includes

- ☑ Mortgage or rent

- ☑ Real Estate Taxes

- ☑ Utilities

☑ Phone

☑ Property Insurance

☑ Equipment

☑ Supplies

☑ Postage

☑ Other Taxes

☑ Losses

☑ Bad Debts

☑ Professional Fees and Services

☑ Publications

Selling Costs

☑ Advertising

☑ Craft Show Fees

☑ Commissions

☑ Photography Costs

- ☑ Printing

- ☑ Travel

- ☑ Meals

- ☑ Credit Card Processing Costs

- ☑ Postage

CHAPTER 7

GETTING ORGANIZED

Setting Up Your Space

One of the most important things you can do in setting up your business is to have a designated space for your work. A room of your own would be ideal, but even a desk or table that is out of the way, where you can spread out and not have to pack up, will work. Don't overlook attics or basements as possibilities. Many home- based business owners tend to try and make do when setting up their workspace. But it's important to have your own designated space that you can tailor to your own needs.

As you begin to set up your workspace, try to visualize all that you will be doing. Decide what furniture and equipment you absolutely need, and what you would like but isn't necessary for startup. I knew someone who converted a large, walk-in closet into an efficient and functional workspace. Be creative, but remember that you need a place where your work can be left undisturbed until you return.

Organize your space and take time up front to gather all your supplies. There is nothing more frustrating than having to run to the kitchen for scissors or a pencil when you're in the middle of a project. Having an established work area with all supplies nearby eliminates wasted time. You will be more productive and able to accomplish more in less time.

Office Space

Will customers be visiting your home office or studio? If so, you will need to project a different kind of image than if you are the only one who ever sees that space.

Consider whether your office is suited to your work, or if home improvements and/or modifications will have to be made. A stained-glass artist or potter will have different space and other requirements than a needlepoint designer.

Will you be content to spend long periods of time in your chosen space? Is it comfortable and will you be motivated and productive while you're there?

Lighting is an important element to consider. Will your space have adequate natural light? Can additional lamps be added to provide enough light? A dark, dreary corner is not inviting, and you won't look forward to spending much time there. So think twice before locating your office/studio in a dark, damp basement. Lighting should provide enough illumination for whatever your craft. It should cast minimal shadows and be bright enough to stimulate you into action rather than lull you to sleep.

Proper furniture is important in your plan. If you will spend a lot of time sitting at a desk or work surface, you should invest in a good chair. Get one that is adjustable, and provides support for your lower back.

There are many choices when it comes to desks. Crafters should consider having a desk in addition to a work surface. Your desk should be used for business paperwork, and can house your phone, computer, printer and other office equipment (if it's big enough). A rule of thumb to determine active area is to sweep your arm across the surface of the desk while you are seated. This is the empty space you'll need to sit and write or pay bills.

Since crafters normally need more work surface than just a desk, consider having another table or similar area for this purpose. I purchased an old library table that works perfectly for me. I can spread out my beads and have enough room to work on several designs without having to pack one up or finish it before doing another.

Other furniture you may want to consider includes a filing cabinet. Along with business paperwork, if you're a designer you will need a space to organize and file your designs. A filing cabinet works better than storage boxes and other more temporary containers. Be sure to check the depth of each drawer, and that you can pull the drawers out all the way. It is difficult to get a file folder from a drawer that only opens three-quarters of the way.

One final furnishing will be shelving space for books, supplies and displays. You may want to consider pre-fabricated shelving units that can be purchased fairly inexpensively. Another choice is to attach the shelves directly to the wall. Be sure they are mounted securely to the studs and can support the weight you intend to put on them.

There are usually three things that come into play when shopping for furniture:

1. Money is normally the first consideration.
   How much is the "perfect" desk? Can you find it used? How about rent to own? Do you have to have this particular furniture, or can another work just as well?

2. Space is another detail, especially if you're confined to sharing space in a room.
   Is there furniture that can have multiple uses? Can you use room divider screens to block off your space? Be sure the furniture you buy will work in the space you've allotted.

3. The final consideration is time.

   How hurried are you to furnish your space? Will you have
   time to shop for a good deal? Or are you willing to pay
   more to get what you want and need without having to shop
   around?

Although it's nice to have everything exactly as you want it at the
outset of your business, this isn't always necessarily required in order to
get your business up and running. Remember, you can invest some of
your profits into better furniture if you're successful.

Before getting out the checkbook, do the following checklist to
identify your precise requirements:

❑ What tasks will you be doing daily? What activities will your
   work require, today and in the immediate future?

❑ What tools and equipment do you need to accomplish those
   tasks? List everything you can think of.

❑ Do you already have some of those tools and equipment? If so,
   cross them off the list. But if there's a better model that would
   increase your production or quality, keep it on the list.

This is your shopping list. Now you can begin to purchase what
you really need.

Supplies

Now that you have furniture, you're going to need some supplies. Here is a partial list to get you started.

Desk Supplies

❑   Stationery, envelopes

❑   Pens, pencils, etc.

❑   Invoice and receipt forms

Promotional Supplies

❑   Business cards

❑   Letterhead

❑   Brochures

Mailing and Shipping Supplies

❑   Boxes

❑   Envelopes

❑   Tape

❑ Stapler

Equipment Supplies

❑ Printer cartridge

❑ Fax toner

❑ Extra disks, CDs, etc.

There are many other supplies that you will need as you begin your new business. Start by making and keeping an ongoing list so you will always know what you need.

Promotional Material Design

In order for your business to appear professional, it will be necessary for you to invest in professional appearing printed materials. Business cards, letterhead, and brochures are a necessary item to your business success.

If you are technically skilled and have a graphic design computer program, you can use an existing template to create your business image. Many office supply stores now carry paper designed for professional use, and by incorporating your design on specialty paper you can achieve a very professional appearance.

If you choose, you can also hire a graphic designer to create an individual logo and design for you. Of course, this will cost a lot more than the do-it-yourself method.

I have personally used my own created design since my business started, printing out a quantity of business cards and other promotional material as needed rather than having to store large quantities from a printer. Also, by having my copy in an electronic format I have the option of e-mailing it or using it in electronic copy.

Crafters have the advantage of people liking the homespun look, and not minding hand lettered tags and brochures. But the more professional you can appear, the better off you will be. Top quality craft shows are looking for professional crafters, not hobbyists.

Business cards are probably one of the first, and one of the most important items you will need. Everyone will want one of your cards, and you will want to hand out as many as possible. I give out business cards all the time, and have them available on my display for anyone to take whether or not they make a purchase. I have gotten calls months later from someone who picked up my card at a craft show and now wanted to make a purchase. I also am careful to include a card with each purchase, along with any other materials I may add.

The variety of business card designs is endless. They can be almost any size, shape, color, or paper you desire. Your business card speaks volumes about your business, and you really need to spend some time thinking about what exactly you want to convey. A business card projects an image of you to a customer, and a favorable image will create a desire to purchase from you.

When designing your card, keep in mind the information you want to include. Your business name along with a line that tells what you do is a good place to start. Don't forget your phone number, including area code. And an e-mail address is useful, along with your website, should you have one. If the design of your card lends itself to it you may want to have a photo of your work on the card. I have also seen some attractive cards that were photographs with the business information printed tastefully around the items shown.

You can be as creative as your budget allows, but you don't have to spend a fortune to have a professional appearance.

Brochures are also an important part of the crafters business promotional materials. As it's not possible for me to send jewelry items out so someone can see it, (unless they care to pay for it first) I send a brochure with photos of my designs out instead. Professional quality photos will go a long way toward making sales.

You want a brochure to explain what you have to offer. It should provide the benefits of your product and convey your overall professionalism. If you can include a few testimonials from others who have been satisfied with their purchases, all the better.

Consider the mood you're trying to convey when choosing what type of paper and what color your brochure should be made of. Paper and color can portray many different feelings and desires. Be sure you send the right message out with yours.

Organizing your Office / Studio

So you've made your home office, and now must find a way to keep everything organized and in some semblance of order. The average person spends 20 minutes a day just looking for things. That adds up to almost 84 hours a year! At $20 an hour, it comes to $1,666 of your time. I don't know about you, but I'd rather not give up that amount of money just because of being unorganized.

You must think about winning the war against paper and clutter at the startup of your business, because if you don't you will be on the road to defeat before you ever begin.

First of all, recognize that correspondence is essential for home-based businesses. Your existence is dependent on getting the word out about your business and products, and getting people to communicate with you. This is done through the mail, both regular and e-mail. Always responding to mail promptly will go a long way toward keeping up with paperwork. But crafters are a unique group, with many other sources of paper entering their lives on a daily basis.

Our attitude about how we control and deal with the paper entering our lives each day has much to do with how we control and deal with it. We are often afraid to part with anything just in case we may need it someday. I know a few folks who even print out all their e-mail and file it, just in case. Rarely is there a time where it is do-or-die without a certain file or letter. I chose early on to eliminate first, and worry later, and have yet to have a major problem. We live in a time of so many resources so easily at our disposal that we rarely can't get something again should we need it.

The best way to handle whatever comes your way is to begin with a system for sorting and handling all incoming items. I began organizing my business files by grouping things into categories. Each of the file categories is then kept in a file drawer or storage container.

I started with an *archive folder* for annual tax records, fictitious name records, and anything else that I won't have to refer to very often.

I keep an *expense folder* for receipts, and keep my *expense / income journal* in this folder, entering each expense item in the journal as it gets filed in the folder. Since I'm in this folder most often, this is where I keep my *Department of Revenue* payment slips for quarterly sales tax payment.

A *bank folder* contains all bank statements, deposits and receipts.

A folder for *craft show information / applications* contains shows I've applied for as well as those I'm thinking about. It also includes tidbits on shows I want to follow up on and comments about shows I've done.

My *design folder* contains copies of each design I've submitted for publication, and a *resources folder* for all the good stuff I want to save that I may need someday.

I have a *submissions folder* that contains correspondence and copies of designs I've sent to be considered for publication. All of these folders are kept in a single file drawer in my desk.

I keep several additional file folders for different purposes. These folders are for *catalogs, patterns and graphs, ideas, tear sheets, writer's guidelines, magazine articles*, and a list of *craft magazines* I can use as a resource.

As you can see, by setting up a file for everything at the start, you will avoid unnecessary clutter and aggravation trying to find whatever you're searching for.

Paperwork never ends, so don't feel guilty about not finishing. Just keep at it and keep up with it so it won't overtake you and your business.

Getting Stocked

Storage soon becomes a prime concern and consideration. After attending my first bead show I discovered how important storage was going to be to the success of my business. As my business grew, I had to decide how to store (and find) raw materials, including the rare glass bead I now need for this design.

I had to decide where to keep all my finished products. I had to organize my design information for submissions, and also needed someplace to keep the magazine articles and other information that could be used in a design or in my business. Then there is the paperwork required for the business as well as for craft shows and design submissions.

Finally, the equipment I need for craft shows also needed to go somewhere. With all this stuff to not only put somewhere, but also be able to find when you need it became a major challenge.

Supplies

I need a large quantity of beads, findings, and other jewelry related materials when I'm designing, because I enjoy trying different sizes, colors and combinations to get a desired effect. But my problem was in trying to locate a particular bead that I knew I had....somewhere. My solution was to invest in a bunch of organizer trays, and to sort all my beads and pearls by color. I usually know what color I'm looking for, even if I can't remember anything else, so this system works best for me. I keep my findings in other trays labeled by what they're for, such as earrings or bracelets or spacers.

Finished Pieces

As I sell at craft shows, how to keep the pieces and transport them to each show was a primary concern. I use a lot of silver and keeping silver clean and untarnished was always a problem. Another concern was security. I would often carry thousands of dollars of inventory by myself to a show and needed a way to keep everything with me or in my locked vehicle. Rubbermaid came to the rescue.

Each of my finished pieces is kept in an airtight, portable Rubbermaid container. The container stays in my car until my display is set up, then I can move and park the car, and take the jewelry back with me to put out. At the end of the show, I pack up the jewelry first and take it with me to the car, along with all the money I made!

At home, as I complete each piece of jewelry I photograph it, price it and put it directly into this container. I always know where everything is.

Inventory Management

Your inventory is like having money in the bank. Finished work that is waiting to be sold is future cash. But in order to know how much money is represented in these pieces, you'll need to keep an inventory record.

Your inventory record should include:

- what the product is

- when it was made

- how much it cost to produce

- where you sold it

- when you sold it

- how much you sold it for

- your profit

- the total number of the same product sold so far

Some crafters prefer to keep their inventory on index cards or in an accounting ledger books, or on computerized programs. A lot depends on what you make. I keep a fairly detailed system for my jewelry designs, as most are one of a kind. I give every piece a number, and calculate the cost of my materials. I try to include an estimate of the amount of time I spent designing and creating each piece, along with a sketch of the piece. When the product sells, I note the date of the sale, where it was sold and the price. I then calculate my profit. If there are multiple pieces of the same design, I also include a quantity number and carry it down when a piece is sold.

Just by looking at my entries I can see my existing inventory as well as what's been sold. In this way I can also track how well I do at any particular craft show or event. At the end of each year I can carry over the existing inventory for tax purposes, and know my sales as well as what my best selling products were.

How much inventory to keep on hand will depend on how actively you market your product. At first it will be a guessing game to try and determine how much you will need, what will sell and what won't, and how much to take with you to a show. But with good records you will soon discover how to manage your inventory to have enough without having too much.

Keeping good inventory records is important. It will give you a lot of useful information. When you've developed a good system, you will find it really doesn't take much time, and the information will prove it's worth the effort.

CHECKLIST - Getting Organized

Office Needs

❑ Telephone: Separate line or cell phone dedicated to business use

❑ Fax machine

❑ Computer: word processing and accounting software, database management, graphic presentation software, Internet access

❑ Filing Cabinets

❑ Desk

❑ Production Table or Workspace

❑ Shelving

❑ Calendars: Planning and Production

CHAPTER 8

TIME / BUSINESS MANAGEMENT

Working Hours

One of the best ways to operate successfully from home is to get organized. Begin by organizing your day. Make a habit of establishing regular working hours. This is your time to create, design, write and craft, and nothing should stop you. If you have small children at home, consider hiring a babysitter or coordinating with another mom for trade off time. Even though this may cost money, it doesn't compare to the amount you would spend for full time childcare if you were working outside the home. And the amount of work you can accomplish during an uninterrupted period of time will be well worth the investment.

While speaking of children, it is very important to set rules about their responsibilities with the business. Younger children must know how to answer the telephone properly, and to be quiet when mom is on the phone. There is nothing more unprofessional than screaming children in the background when trying to conduct business on the phone.

When you are "at work" do not allow unnecessary interruptions. A ringing phone or doorbell does not have to be answered. Caller ID has become a godsend to me. I am able to see if the call is important or just another solicitor. Of course, if my business cell phone rings, it is most likely a customer. So unless I'm at a point where I can't put my work down, I usually answer that line.

When starting my business I purchased a cell phone. The cell phone is my business phone and I use it exclusively for business. This is the number I use on my business cards and stationary, and the number I give to a customer to contact me. I have a nice voice mail greeting for any missed calls, and can return them as soon as possible. The phone is with me always, and I've never had any complaints. To top it off, because I use this phone exclusively for business purposes, the cost is completely tax deductible!

Older children can be an asset to the business. They can understand the economics of having "more money" and are usually more than willing to help. My daughter has assisted in preparation for craft shows and is a great salesperson at the show. She is also one of my best representatives, often wearing and selling my designs to her friends.

Time Management

In order to manage your time you need to simply know everything you have to do and how much time you have to do it in. When you then assign priorities to each item and create a schedule to get it all done, you have addressed and conquered time management.

We all have the same amount of time, so we must learn to use it most productively. To become better managers of our lives and our businesses we have to become better managers of our time.

Good time management practices begin with the following:

4. Look at how you currently spend your time.

5. Decide how you want to spend your time.

6. Control and plan your time.

7. Measure your success or failure.

8. Eliminate time wasters.

Home-based business owners must commit themselves to time management practices. It is too easy to become distracted or sidetracked when you work at home and you constantly have to be on guard to avoid self-sabotage from these distractions. Time wasters such as catching the afternoon soap operas to chatting on the phone can eat into productive time spent reaching your goals. Time management can help.

Every successful businessperson I know is a list maker. If you aren't yet one, start becoming one today. Using a simple list as the start of all your personal and business planning will give you a major advantage.

I'll talk about this more in the next section, but I maintain two lists. The first is a Master List where I enter everything I eventually want to do. This keeps an idea from getting lost, but doesn't mean I have to do it today. My daily task list is just that. Here I list items that I want to finish before my workday is over. I will often have items from the Master list on my daily list, and I may have to break those down into smaller chunks to get them done. But the idea is that I know what I want to accomplish in a given day, and can work toward that end. It also gives me personal satisfaction to cross items off the list as they are completed.

Plan your work and work your plan is an old saying that holds true each day. Effective schedules will help you to accomplish more and avoid leaving things undone.

Simplify For Success

One of the best ways to organize and control your day is to simplify. Keep your life as simple as possible. To do this, you must start by realizing time is a limited resource. You only get so much of it, so decide what is most important and use you time here.

Perfectionism is one of the greatest hindrances of time management, especially for the crafter. Although our products must be perfect, our house can tolerate a bit of dust. If we spend valuable time chasing dust bunnies, we won't have that time to spend crafting. Once you accept the fact that there are areas in your life that can be less than perfect, you will free up a large amount of time.

Begin by writing everything down that you need to remember or do. Always keep a small notebook with you to jot down notes, reminders, and any other things that are pressing. Keep checklists of all you need to do. Write things down so you can free up your brain for more creative pursuits.

Try doing things differently. Just because you've always done something one way doesn't mean it's the best or most efficient way. Look closely at how you manage your business and your home. Can anything be done easier, faster or better? The unconscious habits you have acquired over the years may have worked fine before, but times have changed. So be open to trying new and different ways to do the same old thing.

Setting Goals

Do you really know what you want from your craft business? Do you know what specific aspect of the business inspires and motivates you? Do you know how devoted you want to be to this business? The answers to these questions will help you to begin planning some long-range goals.

Written goals represent the difference between results and good intentions. Setting effective goals will help to motivate you to move ahead, and to reach for something you want. But before starting out, there are a few things you must understand about goals and goal setting.

Goals must be realistic and achievable, and have measurable deadlines. A vague or unrealistic goal will only lead to procrastination, whereas goals should inspire you and guide you to action.

Look at the following goal and see how realistic you think it is:

To make $50,000 by selling my crafts.

This goal is extremely vague and could also be unrealistic. There is too much we don't know. First of all, what is the craft? A high-priced craft may lend itself to this level of income, but selling trinkets probably won't. We also don't know what type of selling the crafter plans to do. Are we talking about craft shows, Internet, co-ops, or what? Another unknown is the time frame for accomplishing when the $50,000 will be earned. Is it for the lifetime of the crafter or for each year? As you can see, there are too many details left unanswered for this to be an effective goal.

But let's see if we can rewrite it to make it clearer. I'll use myself as an example. I make jewelry in the average price range of $45 per piece, with a few much higher priced pieces, and a few inexpensive items. I sell primarily at quality, professional craft shows and I want to earn $50,000 by the end of the year. So my goal would look like this:

> *To sell high-end designer jewelry at professional craft shows*
> *and earn $50,000 by December 31, 20__.*

Now my goal has measurable results. I can see whether I am proceeding toward reaching the goal after each show I do.

As you begin to organize your business, list every goal you hope to achieve. Be as specific as possible, but don't worry yet about the time lines. These are your long-range goals that will set the stage for what you want. By doing this you will help identify exactly what you want to do. Are you most interested in designing pieces or in teaching how to make things? Do you want to sell at craft shows or on the Internet? What really appeals to you?

Your next step is to narrow your list down into smaller, short-term goals and plan how to best proceed to accomplish each of these. Start by identifying three or four goals and making sure they are concise and measurable. Next you can take action steps toward each of these goals every day.

For example, based on what I identified as my goal, I will have to take action on several areas to move toward it. I will have to:

☑ Book enough shows to provide the income I'm seeking

☑ Produce enough merchandise to reach the income level I'm seeking

So I can ask myself what actions can be taken today that will help me reach the goal I have set.

Remember the following when setting goals:

1. Where are you going? Winston Churchill once said, "You can only see as far as you can look." Can you see 18 to 24 months into the future? If so, plan goals out accordingly. Make your goals as specific as possible to get as much from it as possible.

2.   How will you get there? Look at the objectives behind each goal, and see exactly what you will need to do to attain you goals.

3.   How will you know when you've gotten there? Be sure your goal is measurable and that you can mark your progress along the way. A goal isn't a goal unless it can be completed. Be sure you know when the conclusion will occur.

Setting goals is a pretty simple process. Think of it in terms of planning a trip. First you will need to decide where you want to go. Next decide the best way to get there. Watch your progress along the way to be certain you don't get lost. Finally, know when you've arrived. If you look at goals the same way, you will be well on your way.

Planning and Prioritizing

One of the biggest advantages of planning is how it expands the time you have available to do things. It's amazing, but with planning you are able to accomplish so much more.

Planning gives you leverage. Time spent in planning allows you to control more of the balance of your time. It actually gives you free time back. Time-effectiveness studies have concluded that for each minute spent in planning, the time required to complete an activity is reduced by

3 to 4 minutes.   So if you spend 10 minutes planning, you can reduce your completion time by 30 to 40 minutes. I don't know about you, but I could use an additional 30 to 40 minutes in my day.

One of the benefits of planning is that it will help us manage our priorities better.   Planning helps get things done.   It ensures the completion of your priorities and increases your chance of success.

Planning gives direction to energy. You may be excited about what you want to do, but like tires spinning on gravel, you won't go far without a plan.

But many people come up with reasons not to plan. Typically, the day-to-day operations of their life and or business control them rather than the other way around. It's easy to develop the habit of doing things the same way each day, but more productive to challenge everything you do.

Another reason people don't plan is because it lacks immediate gratification. Putting out the fire of the moment does have an immediate reward, but planning could have prevented the fire in the first place.

Many fear planning will increase their workload and the paperwork that may result. They think it will be hard work and don't want to add to an already overloaded schedule. Learning anything new does require a little effort. But the rewards to planning can and will be seen, and will be well worth the effort involved.

Where to Begin

The best place to begin is by determining your personal prime time. Ask yourself what time of day you are at your best. Are you a morning person? Or do you begin to come alive at 10 p.m.? No one operates at the same energy level all the time. Determine when you are at a peak energy level and set a small portion of that time aside to begin planning.

It only takes about 15 minutes a day to plan your work. Identify this time, put it prominently on your calendar, and guard it sacredly.

In order to be most effective, you will need a few tools. A day planner, appointment calendar, Palm Pilot or similar organizer is a necessity. You don't need to spend a fortune on the highest priced, leather bound, diary. But will need to have something that will work for you.

So, once you have your calendar and are at your appointed planning time, you can begin. In goal setting we discussed having a list of long-term goals. Begin with this list to create a Master List of *everything* you ever want to do. It may seem endless, but will capture details that would otherwise escape and be forgotten. Consider your Master List a warehouse for keeping things you want to do eventually.

You may want to divide your Master List into two categories, one for Business related items and one for Personal items. Both are important to your overall success and happiness, so don't allow anything to pass by.

The second list you will create is your Daily Action List. These are items that you will complete today. Schedule these tasks on your calendar and assign them an appointment time to be done. As you review your Daily Action List, consider any projects on your Master List that can be incorporated.

I used to use a daily planner, and have since graduated to a Palm Pilot, to help keep me organized. Every morning I begin my workday by identifying what needs to be done that day. Certain times are reserved for generic business purposes, and others for design and creation. I usually have 4 to 5 items each day that absolutely must be done. I try to do these first to get them out of the way, because my day doesn't end until these items are checked off the list.

My work schedule includes deadlines for each project, and I take these deadlines very seriously. At the end of each day I look at my list to see what I've accomplished, and whether I've done anything that day to help advance my goals.

When I decided to write this book, I had to plan how and when to do it or it would never get done. The book idea was on my Master List and the time was right to get started on it. So my Daily List began to have an appointment time for book work. I began by scheduling time for research and library visits, and then blocked time for writing. Because I do more than just this, if it hadn't been scheduled it would probably never have been written.

Remember, planning is a very individual activity. Only you know what you want or need to accomplish, and only you know how to best accomplish these tasks. So commit to planning how to best use your time and see what happens.

CHECKLIST - Time / Business Management

❑ Do you have regular business hours?

❑ Can you prioritize your tasks and your day?

❑ Do you know how to use various time management tools?

❑ Do you keep a day planner or other electronic organizer?

❑ Do you know how long it takes you to do various business and production tasks?

❑ Do you keep business and personal life separate?

CHAPTER 9

SELLING AT CRAFT SHOWS

The Appeal of Craft Shows

Craft shows are a great way for those just starting out in the craft industry to market their products. Since you are dealing directly with customers, you get immediate feedback – what they like and what they don't. Although this can be a little disconcerting, it does give you an immediate idea whether your craft business will be successful or not.

I became hooked on craft shows from the first one I ever did. I completely enjoyed interacting with customers, listening to their wants and needs, and even taking their advice. I learned a lot about my products and about how much to charge. I also learned by watching other crafters to see what they were doing that made them successful.

Craft shows can be very profitable. Many full time craft business owners make a full time living from selling at craft shows. Where else can you go and get paid to learn about a business you enjoy?

Finding Out About Shows

To find out about where craft shows are being held, start with your local chamber of commerce. They will have information on any fairs or festivals planned that year, and you can then contact the promoter to find out if a craft show will be held in conjunction with the event.

If you attend local craft shows, ask other crafters about upcoming shows. You may also ask local craft shops about any listings they are aware of.

I also depend on several publications to find shows. The following are just a few that you may want to look at to see if they will meet your needs:

Sunshine Artists
1700 Sunset Drive
Longwood, FL 32750

The Crafts Report
700 Orange Street
Wilmington, DE 19801

Where It's At
7204 Bucknell Drive

Austin, Texas 78723

You can find copies of *Sunshine Artist* in local bookstores, and you may be able to request they order a recent issue of the others for you. Each of these publications list hundreds of craft shows throughout the country. Your task will be to choose the right show.

Choosing Shows

Depending on what type of craft show you sell at, you will come in contact with a wide range of customers. Your customers will be various ages and income levels, and will be looking for a certain quality of product. If you have targeted your market and analyzed the type of customer that will want to buy your product, you will know the kinds of shows that will be best for you.

There are basically three types or categories of craft shows. The *Amateur Shows* will include those held by churches, schools and other non-profit organizations. *Professional Shows* are handled through professional promoters, and can be either retail or wholesale. And the *Self-Promoted Shows* can be held by private companies or at home parties at your own or someone else's home. As you gain experience, you should at least try a few shows in each category to see how you like it and how well you do. If you find one is better than the others, stick with it. Otherwise it usually makes sense to keep as many options open as possible. Let's look into each category a little closer.

Amateur Shows are usually organized and run by volunteers. They take care of the site preparation and promotion, and make money for a worthy cause from your entry fee. The volunteers do not personally profit from a show and usually only hold one or two per year.

Church and school shows are a great way to get started in the craft show circuit. Their entry fee is normally low and the people who put them on are usually very nice and helpful, especially if you tell them you're new at this.

At an amateur show you will have fewer restrictions about your display, and will probably be more comfortable than in a show where everyone is a professional. The crafts found at these events can be exceptional to mediocre. Because the church or school is motivated to rent as many spaces as possible, they may allow inferior crafts in the show. Asking other local crafters about different shows will help you to decide whether a show will be a good one or not.

Be sure there will be promotion and outside advertising for the show. Before sending in your application, ask those in charge how they will be promoting the show.

Non-profit organizations often have a greater commitment and understanding of how to make an event successful. They are used to fundraising and know how to promote through advertising.

My very first show was at a local Senior Citizen Center. They provided a table for the display, and I only had to provide a drape and my products. The entry fee was only $15. I met a lot of friendly, helpful people, who gave me all kinds of welcome advice and assistance. I had a great time and was hooked from then on.

Professional Shows are a lot different from those done by volunteers. These shows are handled by a professional show promoter whose profit depends on the success of the shows.

A professional promoter is in the craft show business. He or she handles all aspects of a show, from finding a location for the show to finding the crafters and promoting the show to the public. It's only successful if the crafters are happy with their sales and the customers are happy with the crafts.

Entry fees can be very high at these shows, ranging from a low of $75 to more than $500. And just paying the fee doesn't guarantee you'll be accepted. Competition can be fierce. Only top quality slides or photos will get any consideration.

Normally, crafts displayed at these shows are high quality and higher priced. Customers must often pay an entry fee just for the privilege to shop, so they expect more and are more discriminating.

Another type of professional show is the wholesale show. The most experienced crafters, who either have or can produce a large inventory in a short period of time, should only attempt these shows. Often, when you attend a wholesale show, you will have to trade off your design and creative self with your manufacturing and production self.

Only consider a wholesale show if you are prepared to handle sales volume and have the resources at your disposal to accomplish this. Remember, you will have to purchase materials and supplies up front for all large orders. So time and energy are not the only elements to consider. A cost factor must also be included.

I have never had the interest or desire to participate in a wholesale show as I personally hate to do any production type of work. My bliss comes from the design process and the pleasure of seeing the enjoyment and appreciation on a customers face when they see my designs.

The last show category is the *Self-Promoted Show*. I was invited to participate in my first ever home show a year ago and was pleasantly surprised at the outcome. Five crafters, each having a different craft, displayed our individually priced and labeled items throughout a lovely home. Customers were greeted at the door, and handed a basket to place their purchases.   They could wander and browse, enjoying some refreshments along the way, and then check out at a central location. At the end of the show, each crafter received their earnings. As this show has been going on a while, it is well attended, and that is the secret of its success.

Consider getting together with several other crafters for a home show, but be sure to get the word out. Door prizes are a great way to encourage attendance. And be sure to have everyone sign a guest book so you'll have a mailing list for future shows. Finally, don't limit yourself to Christmas shows alone. Consider having a spring or other occasion shows in addition.

One other alternative is to contact a large business or corporation and see if they will allow a small show to be held on their premises for their employees. If they agree you will probably be allowed to set up for a specific time in their lobby or cafeteria. They may want a fee or payment of some kind, but if they have a large number of employees who will be shopping, it may be worthwhile even with a fee.

If you have good quality products and have taken the time to identify what the best marketing techniques are for your product, gotten to know what your customers want, and select the right kind of show, you can be successful.

Scheduling Shows

When selecting shows to apply to, try to stay close to home. Avoid shows where this is the first show ever held and have no track record. Look for shows where only handcrafted merchandise is being sold, and mass-produced goods are prohibited.

The best thing you can do is to start small. Try to get into a local show, perhaps at a church or similar local event. Take time to get a feel for doing a show before booking too many. Craft shows require a lot of time and effort, so you don't want to overextend yourself without knowing exactly what you're getting in to.

The busiest time of the year for craft shows is from September to December. Many crafters earn half of their money during this period. Beginners often schedule more shows than they can comfortably handle during this time period, and then wear themselves out trying to keep up with production and business management while also attending shows.

Application Process

In order to participate in a craft show you will have to apply for admission. Contact the show promoter and request an application. Fill it out completely and return promptly with your fee and any slides or photographs, which also may be required. Normally your fee will be refunded if you are not accepted into the show. But occasionally shows will charge a small application fee just for reviewing your slides, which is non-refundable. Read the application carefully and always be sure to apply as early as possible, always before the deadline.

As your products will be judged by the quality of your pictures, be sure they are top quality. You may want to consider having professional photos and slides made just for this purpose.

There are several types of shows, and it is important to know the difference between them. Open shows are just that...open to anyone who wants to apply. They have the fewest restrictions on vendors and their products. There are different levels of open shows and you should again try to apply only to those that do not allow the sale of mass-produced merchandise. As a jeweler, I can't compete with jewelry imported from China. And I make no sales when similar products are being sold a row away at less than half of what I'm charging.

Juried shows are more selective. When you apply to a juried show, your photos will be reviewed by a committee to try and determine the quality of your products. They will also consider how many other crafters are applying within the same craft category. A well balanced show wants everyone to profit, and will not have too many of any one craft on display. The jury will be very selective, and will try to pick who they think is the best from each category. Juried shows are sometimes

hard to get in to. But if you are rejected, don't take it personally.
Review your slides to be sure they are the best they can be, and plan on
applying again next year. I have had to wait three years to get into a
show I really wanted. It was worth the wait.

Confirmation and Instructions

After sending your application in, you will have to wait to see if you
are accepted. Normally you will receive a written confirmation or
rejection within a few weeks after the deadline has passed. If you don't
receive some type of notification within a reasonable period after the
application deadline has passed, contact the show promoter. I once
applied to a show that held my application, without notifying me, just in
case one of their first picks cancelled. This kept me from applying for
another show for that same date. When I called and found out what they
were doing, I withdrew my application. This practice is completely
unfair to crafters, and I will not apply to shows that do this. It's ok to
remain on a waiting list if you know about it, but not to be held in limbo
when you may have other options available.

When you receive your confirmation, you will also receive show
instructions. These will tell you what time you can begin to set up your
display, where to park when you are loading and unloading, where to
park during the show, and any other special requirements the promoters
may require. Be prepared for some special requirements for each show

and try to remain flexible and creative. Solutions can be figured out for all situations.

Booth Space

Depending on the size of the show, you may be told where your booth will be located. But most often you won't know this until you check in.

The space you will be allotted is usually advertised in the information that is sent with your application, so there shouldn't be any surprises. Most outside displays allow at least a 10' X 10' space, which is the standard size of most professional canopies. If you have extra space, say 10' X 12", you will probably be allowed to display some of your merchandise outside of the confines of your canopy. The space allotments for inside shows will range from a small 6' X 8' to a generous 12' X 12'. When selecting shows, keep in mind that larger booth space will allow more room to display your products.

Unless otherwise specified, you are responsible for providing your own tables and display materials. You will need table coverings that reach the floor. If tables will be provided, be sure to find out their size ahead of time. I was once surprised at a show to find out that the tables which were provided were 10' long! My table coverings didn't fit. The show promoter helped me improvise, but I wasn't happy with the overall look of my display for that show. Lesson learned....always take all of your own materials. Even if they never get used, at least they're there if you need them.

Supplies

There are some essential items in addition to tables and coverings that you must have at craft shows. I keep everything I need for shows in a large plastic container. This way, I don't have to think about it, but can just grab the container when I'm packing the car for a show.

These essentials include:

- ☑ Your sales tax certificate

- ☑ Receipt book and pens

- ☑ Calculator

- ☑ Business cards

- ☑ Mailing list book

- ☑ Order forms for additional merchandise

- ☑ Extra product labels and tags

- ☑ Gift boxes and bags

☑ Display signs

☑ Safety pins, tape and a small stapler

☑ Credit card imprint machine and forms

☑ Display equipment and accessories (such as racks, decorative scarves, or boxes)

☑ Product repair kit (I keep pliers, jewelers glue, and other items of this nature together in a small container)

☑ Money – change for purchases made

By gathering all your miscellaneous supplies and keeping them together, you will always be prepared.

Displaying your Products

Your display is probably the single most important item to your success at a craft show, and you should spend time trying to make it as professional and attractive as possible. How you present your products has a direct bearing on how much you will make.

The display should be eye-catching and neat. If customers can't see your products, they can't buy them, so keep it uncluttered. Try to make use of all your booth space. Think of ways to place items both horizontally and vertically. I hang clothing around my booth to display how my jewelry will look, and often end up selling items off of a display. Keep your booth interesting so customers will want to keep looking at your products and not have their eyes wander to another booth that catches their attention.

The hardest thing in the beginning, but most important, is to have enough inventory for each show you book. As the period between Labor Day and Christmas are the busiest for craft shows, you may find yourself working overtime to have enough products to fill your display.

But remember, there is a fine line between having a full display and having a clutter of too many items. Sometimes if too much stuff is put out, customers are overwhelmed and can't decide.

When I first started out, I would try to put every single item in my inventory out on display. I had hundreds of pins, necklaces almost piled on top of each other, bracelets and earrings scattered from one end of my table to the other. After observing how other crafters displayed their jewelry, I changed my tactics. I now try to make sets of jewelry to include a necklace, bracelet and earrings. Each are for sale individually, but are discounted if purchased in a set. I display several sets along with unique individual pieces. When a piece or set is sold, I replenish it from additional inventory I keep under my display table. My sales increased considerably when I changed my approach.

Other Equipment

We talked a little about supplies that you will need for shows, but you will also need some additional equipment. Some is more expensive than others, but you may be able to make purchases at discount clubs such as Sam's Club, or find creative uses for furniture found at garage sales and flea markets.

Your display tables will be hauled in and out of many shows, so be sure you get ones that you can carry and aren't too heavy. Most are 6' X 2' or 6' X 3', and are folding. A small card table is also handy to have for expanding your display or for writing up and packaging purchases.

Tables must be covered to the floor. You may start out by using large tablecloths, or you may want to purchase prefabricated table drapes. I wanted something unique, and ended up finding a large, banquet sized tablecloth that was perfect. With my limited sewing ability I was able to stitch up the sides to hang properly, and now have a beautiful display cloth.

Layering on your display table adds to its attractiveness. My covering is a deep burgundy, so I use black velvet pieces on top to place my jewelry. The colors draw customers to my booth.

As you are beginning to make purchases, don't forget a folding chair. Most shows prohibit lawn chairs, and the preference is generally a director's chair.

Other display items you may want to consider include shelving, lattice, racks, and crates or boxes. Depending on your craft, you may need some of these items to best display your products. Crates can serve a dual purpose by being used to pack and carry stuff to and from your car, and also used in your display. Remember, any display items will have to be hauled to and from your vehicle. So avoid very bulky and heavy items.

For outdoor shows you will need a tent or canopy. Although you may think a canopy is optional, after your first show in the rain you will understand how important one really is. Entry fees are usually not refundable because of rain, so if you forfeit the show, you will forfeit your fee. Also, the promoter may not accept you in the future if you don't show up or leave early due to bad weather. Again, the standard size is 10' X 10", which fits nicely in most allotted show spaces. I would suggest you go for the professional EZ Up type of canopy instead of the cheaper kinds you can find at most discount stores. These are umbrella type canopies that are fairly easy to set up (with some practice) and have sidewalls that come in very handy for wind, rain, and obnoxious neighbors.

After playing with many different options for tying my canopy down in windy conditions I discovered what I think is the perfect solution. I use deflateable water containers. You can purchase four of these at any camping supply store. Just fill them with water when you arrive and tie one at each corner of your canopy. When the show is over, dump the water and you're ready to go. They take up no room and are a lot lighter to haul than sandbags or cement blocks.

Targeting Your Market

Do you know who would want to purchase what you make? In order to know who your customers are, you need to find out the following:

➢ What is the age and sex of my customers?

➢ Will they purchase my products for themselves or as a gift?

➢ What would they use it for?

➢ What is the income level of customers who will purchase my products?

This information will help you target what type of show would be best. If you use high priced materials and must charge more for your products, you will not want to do a show in a low-income area, or do a small, homespun show where the other crafts are very inexpensive.

Try to form a customer profile, and then tailor your products to those customers.

Dealing with Customers

When a customer arrives at your booth, your initial attitude and greeting will do much toward whether or not a purchase is made. Always greet your customers. Smile! Say "good-morning", "good-afternoon", "isn't it a beautiful day", "a hot day", "a cold day", I like the _____ you're wearing"....whatever! Try to engage them in enough of a conversation to keep them looking a while and finding out you're a nice person. People want to deal with nice people.

If a customer shows an interest in a particular piece, try to tell them something about it. What it's made of, or if it's an original design or one of a kind will be an enticement. Don't pounce on a customer, but be engaged and helpful.

Don't ever sit back and read a book at a craft show. If you're not interested in what you're selling, why should anyone else be interested? Always try to look busy. Spend time rearranging or straightening your products, fold brochures, stack business cards, do something to look active and interested.

One thing you will soon discover about craft shows is that customers are drawn to booths with customers in them. Customers are like magnets to other customers. If my booth is empty, I walk in front of it and arrange and straighten my stock. It must appear that I'm shopping because soon others come over to look. Try it. It really works!

Marketing Techniques

In order to be successful as a crafter, you must do more than make a good product. You must also market them effectively. Some marketing techniques at craft shows include what your display looks like, how you package your products, and how you present them and yourself at a show.

There are a few marketing tips that you can consider when looking for ways to add value to your work. Occasionally people need a little encouragement to decide to buy your product. Your job is to give it to them and one way to do this is to somehow make your product special.

You can do this in a number of ways. You can sign each piece or several special pieces. A limited edition series or series of collectables that can be added to, with a new design each year is another way to draw interest and value to your work. As I personally don't like to do production work, my jewelry designs tend to be unique and often one-of-a-kind. I stress this to my customers if they stop and admire a particular piece. In today's world of cookie-cutter designs, people seem to appreciate having the only one of something.

Other ways to market at craft shows is to demonstrate your talents. Describe the technique or process as you are creating. If your product lends itself to this, show how to use it.

Making beaded jewelry is difficult to do during a show. I know others who are able to create pieces while chatting with passers-by, but I am unable to focus on a design and on my customers at the same time. I am also not fond of chasing beads across the display floor. So instead of demonstrating, I wear a few of my better pieces and try as much as possible to get the customers to try on the pieces they stop to admire. I keep a tabletop mirror on my display, and encourage anyone who picks something up to try it on. If they try it on they are much more inclined to take it home.

If there is anything unusual about any piece, be sure to add a small tag or card to the item that explains why it is special. I use unusual semi-precious stones in many of my designs, so I will put a tag on the piece telling what the stones are. I will also have a small, standardized card, which gives some information about all the gemstones I use which I offer to anyone making a purchase. Educating my customers about the gems in various pieces often entices them to increase their purchase.

Packaging

Think about the best way to send your product home with a customer after a purchase. Supermarket bags are not a professional way to end a sale.

You will have to consider the size of your product, along with the cost of any packaging material. Boxes and decorative paper bags are nice, but more expensive than you may want to consider. Larger items such as floral arrangements can be wrapped in sheets of tissue paper. Clear plastic bags with a little bit of colored tissue paper can be a good way to send most purchases home.

Show Security

Keep your money in a safe place during the show and don't count your money until after the show is over and you are safely at home.

Many crafters use a cash box, and this works well if there are at least two people managing your booth. But this can be a problem if you are doing a show alone. It's a sorry world we live in, but I've heard horror stories of two customers working together, one to distract the crafter while the other liberates the cash box. Whether I have help or not, I keep my cash in a fanny pack secured to my waist during the entire show. I move large bills and checks to a different compartment of the fanny pack, and keep change in the large, center compartment.

When making change, be sure to leave the bill the customer gives you out and in sight until after you provide the change. This will prevent a customer from thinking they handed you a hundred dollar bill instead of a twenty.

Security is another issue to consider at shows. If you have small products such as jewelry or miniatures, you will have a greater risk of theft. Try to keep your most expensive pieces at the back of your display, closer to you. At an exceptionally busy show, try to have a helper to keep watch while you complete a sale. Theft of small items, especially jewelry, is almost inevitable. Be sure to have an accurate inventory at the start of each show and do a closing inventory after the show to see if you had any losses. If so, the loss can be written off of taxes, which is a small consolation for the time lost. I used to worry about theft, but now feel that if someone steals one of my pieces, they will have to answer to the Lord, not me.

Remember that craft shows are not flea markets. Prices are not negotiable. Have faith in your work and in its quality, and don't give in to haggling over the prices you have set. I already provide a discount for purchasing a set, and will also give a discount for an exceptionally large purchase. But that's as far as I go. I know my work will sell eventually, if not at this show than at another.

Show Evaluation

After doing a show, you will need to decide whether or not it was a worthwhile experience and whether you would do it again. Things to consider will include how much it cost to do the show. Was the application fee reasonable and what were your costs to travel to the show? How many hours did you devote to the actual show and any travel to and from the show? Did many customers attend? What was the purchasing attitude like? Was buying heavy overall, or were most attendees just looking? What was the quality of the overall products in the show? Were they mediocre or a great value for the money? Were you satisfied with your sales?

Be careful when asking others if they felt a show was good. Their scale of what's good may be far different from yours. Some may consider a $100 show a good one, while others may think a $500 show was only average.

There are some industry standards that you may want to consult. To be an excellent show, a crafter should sell more than ten times the cost of the booth space. A good show would result in sales of ten times the booth space, and a fair show would have sales only six to nine times the cost of the booth space. A poor show would have sales less than six times the booth fee.

So if a show cost $50 to enter, you should have the following gross sales to demonstrate the ranking of the show for each category:

Excellent - $500+
Good - $450 - $500
Fair - $300 - $449
Poor - $0 – 299

When using this formula you need to consider some other things. Was the show a one-day or two-day show? Are your items priced at the low end or upper end? If you sell relatively inexpensive pieces, it would be hard to justify the above formula with any accuracy.

Remember, these are only guidelines, and only you will know whether a show was profitable or not. You know how much you need to cover your expenses and make a profit, and if you are happy, don't rule out doing a show again because you didn't meet the industry standards.

CHECKLIST - Selling at Craft Shows

Packing for a Craft Show

❑ Tables and booth display

❑ Chairs

❑ Extension cords

❑ Lighting and extra bulbs

❑ Trash bag

❑ Canopy or Tent

❑ Duct tape

❑ Small tool box

❑ First aid kit including aspirin

❑ Small office supply kit

❑ Cash box and change

❑ Receipt book

❑ Credit Card Processing equipment

❑ Business Cards

❑ Brochures

❑ Price Tags

❑ Guest book for mailing list

❑ Signs for your products

❑ Display aids

❑ Cards which list other shows where you will be participating

❑ Product repair kit, if applicable

❑ Cooler and thermos with food and drink

❑ Sweater or jacket

❑ Tissues

❑ Selected Inventory you plan to sell

❑ Other

_____

_____

How to Select a Show

Ask the following:

- Does jury, invitation or first come make the show selection?

- When will you be notified of acceptance or rejection?

- How many years has this show been held?

- How many applications were received last year?

- How many applicants are expected to return?

- How many new applicants will be accepted?

- What is the space fee?

- What was last year's attendance?

- What advertising for the show is done?

- Is there an entry fee for customers?

- Are craft categories limited?

- What is the price range of crafts at this show?

- Does the show allow, encourage, forbid demonstrations?

- If an outdoor show, what is the policy for bad weather?

CHAPTER 10

OTHER WAYS TO PROFIT

FROM YOUR DESIGNS

Although craft shows are my primary source of revenue for the sale of my jewelry, there are other ways to profit. In fact, you can have a thriving crafts business without ever leaving home. You can sell in retail stores and gift shops, on the Internet, and by direct mail.

The more ways you have to sell your crafts and the more you will sell, the greater your profit. Remember as we explore the following options, that stores will want to purchase your products at wholesale costs, so be sure you can still realize a good profit if you choose to sell in this manner.

Selling Finished Products

Retail and Wholesale

By having your products on display in a gift shop or retail store, you will have greater exposure over a longer period of time. Stores offer great exposure for your products. It is available for sale whenever the store is open, and you don't have to be there to make a sale.

When choosing a store, look for one that your product will complement. How will your product look on their shelves along with other products displayed there? Gift shops and specialty stores are usually a good bet, but always keep your eyes open for other possibilities. I found a small kitchen oriented store called Faith in the Kitchen. They were Christian oriented, and loved my "cooking angels." You never know until you ask. And all they can say is "no thanks".

Some other shops include hospital gift shops, museum and corporate gift shops, antique stores, and even framing and photo stores, depending on your product. Don't overlook anything. Stores are always looking for new products to sell, and you may be doing them a favor by offering the perfect product. Just be sure you can meet their inventory needs when they place an order!

When you locate a store where you think your product would fit well, make an appointment with the owner. Arrive dressed in a businesslike manner, with samples of your product and a prepared presentation of what you're selling and for how much, and why you think the people that shop at that store would want to buy your product.

Stress the benefits to the store and their customers. Does your product satisfy a need? If so, explain how.

Many storeowners are reluctant to do business with those they consider small time operators. They are afraid of being stuck with inferior merchandise or merchandise they order and never receive. Help them overcome this reluctance and do whatever you can to build confidence in you and your product. Take business cards and brochures with you, and even if the owner decides not to make a purchase at this time you can leave something behind for them to review and consider. Always follow up with a thank you note to the owner, and put them on your mailing list to send periodic information. If they see you are moving forward in your business and staying in business, they may become a customer.

The first order is always the hardest, but if you have confidence in your product, don't give up. You will get that order and many more will follow.

Consignment Sales

Selling on consignment means leaving your products at a store, but not getting paid until your product sells. If the item never sells, you never get any money for it. Sometimes consignment arrangements turn into direct sales relationships, if your products have proven to be marketable and you are reliable in supplying the store with sufficient inventory.

How much you will earn with consignment sales is based on a predetermined commission. Normally the commission is somewhere between 40 – 60% of the retail price, and consignments are usually paid at the end of each month for the previous month's sales.

It is important that you keep your prices consistent, especially if you sell at more than one store in the same general area. Additionally, you should offer to make an appointment to visit the store periodically to replenish your stock and show any new products you may have.

Selling by consignment has its good points and bad. It is time consuming. You have to keep track of inventory that is not in your possession, but not yet sold. You will have money (hopefully) due you that you won't be able to lay hands on until the following month. You may have pieces returned due to damage, which you will need to spend additional time repairing. But still many crafters find consignment sales very profitable and rewarding, and choose it as their main source of income.

If you decide to sell on consignment, be sure all of the details are agreed upon up front. This will save a lot of potential hassles down the road.

Using Sales Representatives

If you want to spend more time designing and producing your crafts, and less time marketing, you may want to consider hiring a salesperson to do this for you. In fact, you may want to hire several to really make a sales impact.

One of the biggest advantages of hiring a sales representative is that they already are established with storeowners and others that purchase what you're trying to sell. They have an existing network of contacts, and have a rapport with many different types of shops and shop owners.

A good sales representative can give you valuable feedback on the marketplace, on what's selling and what's not. They can give you advice you may not have thought of, and can help make you successful. After all, they only make money if your product sells, so it's in their best interest to help you succeed.

So how do you find a good sales representative? A good way to start is by visiting local shops and galleries, and asking the storeowner for the name of their salesperson for handcrafts. You may want to explain that you produce handcrafts that you think would complement their merchandise. Normally, storeowners are glad to provide this information.

Contact the sales rep and see if she is accepting new products. Find out what her commission rate is and how many stores she services. You will also want to know the geographic area and what types of stores she calls on. You don't need to be located in the same area as the sales rep in order for them to represent you. In fact, it is a benefit to have your products marketed in areas you may not have easy access to.

If the sales rep is willing, send photos and samples of your products for their consideration. I would enclose return postage if the sales rep doesn't think it is something they want to carry. The Internet comes in very handy during this time, and you can direct the rep to your web site if you have one, or offer to email photos of your products directly to the rep with samples to follow. If she agrees to represent you, you will need to sign an agreement outlining the responsibilities of each party. The sales rep will most likely have a standard contract that you can review and modify as needed to suit your needs.

Selling through a sales rep is a convenient way to sell your product wholesale. The salesperson visits the stores and takes orders and sends the orders to you. You will then ship the products directly to the store and either include an invoice or COD payment. When their check clears the bank you send the sales rep a check for their commission. Try to arrange all commissions be paid at one time, perhaps at the end of the month, for all sales made that month. That will save paperwork and having to write several checks.

It is important to always remain professional in your dealings with your sales representatives. Treat them well, pay them on time, and stand behind your products. In turn, they will serve you well and provide you with many sales you may never have had an opportunity to make on your own.

Cooperative Craft Shops

One of the latest trends in selling crafts is the cooperative or co-op craft shop. These are usually buildings devoted to handcrafted merchandise only.

This type of co-op works by each crafter committing to display their crafts, either in a designated area or mixed among other crafts in the store, and by paying a monthly fee to cover overhead. The fee may be calculated by how much product you have and how much space you'll need. An additional commission on sales may also be charged.

Be careful when entering into this type of agreement. Read the fine print or consult with your attorney. There may be other requirements involved that you are unaware of, and suddenly responsible for. You may be required to spend a certain amount of time at the store, or to demonstrate your craft. That may not be a problem, but you'll need to know up front if you are required to be there on Saturday mornings, when you have craft shows scheduled.

The agreement or contract will be for a specified period of time, and you should try to negotiate the shortest period of time possible for your first try. You will have inventory tied up and need to know how quickly it will move. If your products don't sell, you will still have to leave them there until the end of the agreement.

Check to see the advertising policy of the co-op. Do they get the word out that it exists? No one will come if they don't know it's there. Talk to others whose work is in the co-op and see how satisfied they are. Does their work sell? Are they happy with the proprietors? Are they paid on time?

Selling at co-ops can be profitable. But be sure you know exactly what you are getting in to before you sign.

Advertising and Direct Mail Sales

Many crafters enjoy making their products, and want or need to make money, but don't want to deal directly with customers. If you fall into this category, you may want to consider selling items by direct mail.

Some of the options available to you include advertising your products in magazines and in catalogs of handcrafted products. If this appeals to you, begin by researching what type of magazine would be a good place to sell your merchandise. Avoid craft "how-to" magazines, as the people who purchase them usually would prefer to make their own items than to purchase the completed project. You should also research the type of catalog that may be a good one to host your projects.

The library is a good place to start. Your librarian can point you to periodicals that list all types of catalogs as well as magazines. Get copies of these and see what similar products are being sold and how much they sell for.

You will want to find out advertising rates for each publication. Many will offer a discount for multiple listings, but try not to pay for too many ads up front. As with co-op selling, you won't know how well your product will do until after you try it. So start small and see what happens.

One of the advantages of direct marketing is that you control your inventory until it is sold. You should be sure you have enough inventory on hand, or have the potential to produce additional pieces should you get flooded with orders.

There are some specific regulations you need to know when selling by mail. Orders must be filled within a certain period of time, or money refunded. Be sure you understand all that is required.

Direct mail is an efficient way to market your products and can be used creatively in many ways. I always include an order sheet of a few of my most popular pieces with every purchase made at craft shows.

This way, when a customer gets home and realizes she need one more angel pin for Aunt Agnes, she can just pop the order form in the mail, knowing she'll have it in a week. This provides a lot of ongoing business, and income, after each show.

There are other creative ways to market your products, and you should continually be looking into each one. The Internet is phenomenal, and I intend to write an entire book about selling your handcrafts online. Just remember to use every opportunity to promote and market your work, and continually seek out new and different ways, and you will be successful!

CHECKLIST - Other Ways to Profit

How to find new Markets for your Products

- Brainstorm ways to find new audiences

- Obtain customer information and learn how to use it

- Spend time wisely, more on production and less on business management

- Watch what others do and copy them

- Learn to teach what you know

- Consider becoming a retailer

- Travel to new areas and locations with your items

- Diversify your selling methods

- Become more creative in using retailing techniques

RESOURCES

Publications

Accent Magazine
485 7th Avenue #1400
New York, NY 10018
212-594-0880

Accessories Magazine
PO Box 5550
Norwalk, CT 06856
203-853-6015

Accessory Merchandising
400 Knightsbridge Pkwy.
Lincolnshire, IL 60069
800-621-2845

ACF News
PO Box 476
Glenshaw, PA 15116
412-487-7715

American Craft Magazine
72 Spring St.
New York, NY 10012
212-274-0630

**American Jewelry
Manufacturer Magazine**
One State St. 6th Floor
Providence, RI 02908
401-274-3840

American Glass Review
PO Box 2147
Clifton, NJ 07015
973-779-1600

**American Woodworker
Magazine**
33 East Minor St.
Emmaus, PA 18098
610-967-8029

American Style Magazine
3000 Chestnut Ave.
Baltimore, MD 21211
410-235-5116

Art Calendar Magazine
PO Box 199
Upper Fairmount, MD 21867
410-651-9150

Art in America
575 Broadway, 5th Floor
New York, NY 10012
212-941-2800

Artforum
65 Bleeker St.
New York, NY 10012
212-475-4000
ARTnews
48 W. 38th St.
New York, NY 10018
212-398-1690

Art / Quilt Magazine
PO Box 630927
Houston, TX 77263
713-978-7054

Ceramics Monthly
PO Box 12788
1609 Northwest Blvd.
Westerville, OH 43212
614-895-4212

Colored Stone Magazine
60 Chestnut Ave. #201
Devon, PA 19333
610-293-1112

Country Business Magazine
707 Kautz Rd.
St. Charles, IL 60174
630-377-8000

The Crafts Report
PO Box 1992
300 Water St.
Wilmington, DE 19899
302-656-2209

Décor Magazine
330 N. 4th St.
St. Louis, MO 63102
314-421-5445
Fashion Jewelry Magazine
100 Wells Ave.
Newton, MA 02159
617-964-5100

FiberArts Magazine
50 College St.
Asheville, NC 28801
704-253-0467

Fine Woodworking Magazine
PO Box 5506
Newtown, CT 06470
203-426-8171

**Gifts & Decorative
Accessories Magazine**
51 Madison Ave.
New York, NY 10010
212-689-4411

Giftware News
PO Box 5398
112 Adrossan Ct.
Deptford, NJ 08096

Gift & Stationery Business Magazine
One Penn Plaza, 10th Floor
New York, NY 10019
800-950-1314

Glass Art Magazine
PO Box 260377
Highlands Ranch, CO 80126
303-791-8998

Glass Craftsman Magazine
PO Box 678
Richboro, PA 18954
215-860-9947

The Guild
931 E. Main St. #108
Madison, WI 53703
800-969-1556

Home Furniture Magazine
630 S. Main St.
PO Box 5506
Newtown, CT 06407
800-926-8776

Home Magazine
1633 Broadway, 44th Floor
New York, NY 10019
212-767-6810

Home Accents Today
7025 Albert Pick Rd.
Suite 200
Greensboro, NC 27409
910-605-0121

Home Lighting & Accessories
1011 Cliffton Ave.
Clifton, NJ 07013
973-779-1600

Home Textiles Today Magazine
245 W. 17th St.
New York, NY 10011
212-337-6900

Interior Design Magazine
249 W. 17th St.
New York, NY 10016
212-645-0067

Interiors & Sources Magazine
666 Dundee Rd. Ste 807
Northbrook, IL 60062
847-498-9880

Interweave Press
201 E. 5th St.
Loveland, CO 80357
970-669-7672

Jewelers' Circular Keystone Magazine
201 King of Prussia Rd.
Radnor, PA 19089
610-964-4474

Jeweler's Resource Bureau
129 Secor Lane
Pelham Manor, NY 10803
914-738-8485

Kitchenware News
PO Box 1056
Yarmouth, ME 04096
207-846-0600
LDB Interior Textiles
342 Madison Ave.
New York, NY 10173
212-532-9290

Lapidary Journal
60 Chestnut Ave. #201
Devon, PA 19333
610-293-1112

Marketing Directions
7805 Telegraph Rd. #215
Minneapolis, MN 55438
612-944-6805

Metalsmith Magazine
5009 Londonderry Dr.
Tampa, FL 33647
813-977-5326

Metropolis Magazine
177 E. 87th St.
New York, NY 10028
212-722-5050

Modern Jeweler Magazine
445 Broad Hollow Rd. #21
Mellville, NY 11747
516-845-2700

Museums and More
3525 Del Mar Heights
Rd. #200
San Diego, CA 92130
800-538-6673

Niche Magazine
300 Chestnut Ave. Suite 304
Baltimore, MD 21211
410-889-3093

Ornament Magazine
PO Box 2349
San Marcos, CA 92079
760-599-0222

Pottery Making Illustrated
PO Box 6136
Westerville, OH 43086
614-794-5809

Shuttle, Spindle & Dyepot Magazine
3327 Duluth Hwy.
Duluth, GA 30096
770-495-7702

Southern Arts & Crafts
PO Box 159
Bogalusa, LA 70427
504-732-5616

Stained Glass
6 So. West 2nd St. Ste. 7
Lee's Summit, MO 64063
800-438-9581

Stores Magazine
325 7th St. NW
Washington, DC 20004
202-628-8103

Studio Potter Network
41 Neal Mill Rd.
Newmarket, NH 03857
603-659-2632

Sunshine Artist Magazine
2600 Temple Dr.
Winter Park, FL 32789
800-597-2573

Threads Magazine
63 S. Main St.
Newtown, CT 06470
203-426-8171

Visual Merchandising & Store
Design
407 Gilbert Ave.
Cincinnati, OH 45202
513-421-2050

Watch & Clock Review
Magazine
2403 Champa
Denver, CO 80205
303-296-1600

Where It's At
7204 Bucknell Dr.
Austin, TX 78723

Woodshop News
35 Pratt St.
Essex, CT 06426
860-767-8227

Woodworker West
PO Box 66751
Los Angeles, CA 90066

Look for my new book coming soon!

How to Make Money at Craft Shows

Printed in the United Kingdom
by Lightning Source UK Ltd.
9814100001B/52